Waiting for the Light

Daily Reflections for Advent and Christmas

Compiled by Susan Wade, Ricci Kilmer, and Christine Sine

Mustard Seed Associates

2011 © Mustard Seed Associates
www.msainfo.us

Join us in creating the future one mustard seed at a time.

Mustard Seed Associates
P.O. Box 45867
Seattle, WA 98115

©2011 by Mustard Seed Associates

Cover design; Judy Naegeli
Cover photo (c) Christine Sine

To bloggers across the globe who love God and are passionate about sharing their faith in order to reach out to others who are searching for a deeper walk with God.

Table of Contents

Introduction

① If that is my anticipation - the confidence that, there is a purpose-filled & glorious end to "time" as I know it now, my focus must be regularly corrected: Is the way that I am thinking, speaking, living a witness to our Creator God's ways. Am I yielded to Father's redemptive purposes & ready to be transformed by His indwelling Spirit - a living witness to His graciousness that invites all who would come to "Come"?

Advent: A Season of Preparation

Advent marks the beginning of the liturgical year. This is not only meant to be a season of refreshment and renewal but also one of reflection and refocusing, as we anticipate the birth of Jesus, the one who brings life and meaning to all we are and do. In this season we all await the coming of Christ in quiet expectation. It is not just a memorial of his coming to us as a baby 2,000 years ago. We also wait in hope for his coming into lives today as Savior and Lord. Above all, we await in breathless anticipation his coming again at the end of time when the fullness of God's redemption will be revealed and all creation will indeed be made new. ①

Preparing our hearts for God's eternal world in which all things will be transformed and made new is about more than just living good lives and waiting for Christ's return. We are invited to enter into the truth of God-incarnate by allowing Jesus' life, death and resurrection to transform for our own lives as we move incarnationally into the purposes of God.

The hectic days leading up to Christmas can overwhelm us. So can the brokenness and need in the world and our limited ability to speak and act into that need. The reality of Christ incarnate makes possible the planting of little mustard seeds of hope, joy, celebration, healing, and reconciliation all over the world; seemingly insignificant acts emerging, growing, and becoming far more than we can ever ask or imagine.

May Redemption have its perfect work in me for a purpose. May my mind may be deeply & truly transformed & renewed & my bodily life demonstrate that fact

I'm have redeemed me for a purpose.

give our "gifts"/acts to Jesus first & remember the little boy's lunch that Jesus multiplied.

Tom and I set up an Advent wreath on the dining room table each year on the first day of Advent. Four bright red candles nestle in a bed of greenery around a central white candle. At breakfast each morning we light the appropriate candles, symbolic of the fact that Christ is our light in the darkness of the world. During the first week of Advent only one candle is lit. Then a fresh candle is lit each week until on Christmas Day all the candles are set ablaze to welcome Christ. Their brightness shines over our breakfast table throughout the twelve days of Christmas. As the candles burn brightly, we read the daily scriptures from the Book of Common Prayer, focusing on our anticipation of the coming of Christmas and our celebration of Christ's birth. At this busy season of the year this short ritual helps us refocus our energy beyond the consumer culture to center on our faith. It brings tremendous refreshment and renewal to our spirits.

We also like to go on a prayer retreat during Advent. We get away for a couple of days to reflect on what we believe to be God's call on our lives. We review our sense of God's call on our lives and set goals for the next year that flow out of our understanding of God's purpose for us. Prayer retreats like this are an important priority for us. They help us to keep focused on God's purposes rather than our own desires and ambitions and enable us to accomplish all that God intends for us to do.

In the Northern hemisphere Advent begins at the darkest time of the year. As the short days of winter quietly steal upon us God's creation slows down and seems to sleep. Under its covering of leaves or snow it rests and waits for the coming of spring and the growth of a new year. This is the season when plants put down deep roots that anchor them and provide nourishment through the droughts and storms of the coming year.

Advent is a time for us too to slow down, to watch, reflect and refocus as we wait and prepare ourselves for the coming of Christ our Savior and Redeemer into the world. During this season we should set aside time to reflect on our faith. We too need deep roots that provide solid foundations for our life

Thy will be done on earth as it is in heaven

and anchor us against the storms and droughts that may lie ahead.

Whether or not you're familiar with the season of Advent, we invite you to slow down with us. Take more time to reflect on the meaning of God-incarnate, and find new ways to celebrate the tremendous gift of God and the new possibilities opened up for us, and our world, by the coming of Jesus.

Christmas: The Reason for the Season

Though we may not have heard of Advent, all of us know about Christmas and the celebration of Christ's birth. Christmas is probably the most widely celebrated Christian festival in the world. Incredibly, the birth of a tiny baby two thousand years ago in an obscure village in Palestine still has the power to transform lives.

Unfortunately it is also the most commercialized event on our calendars and even for many Christians is fast losing its religious significance. My friend Robyn hates Christmas. "I eat too much, drink too much and constantly rush from one store to another, afraid that I have forgotten to buy a gift for someone important. The fact that we are celebrating the birth of Christ hardly even registers on my screen."

How many of us, like Robyn, feel that we have been duped but find it difficult to move beyond the commercial hype to the true meaning of Christmas? What should be an ideal opportunity to teach simplicity and the foundations of our faith to our children has become one of the greatest displays of materialism and consumer society. How do we escape its insidious pressures?

Christians should never lose sight of the fact that we are celebrating the birth of our Savior into the world. Don't try to out party the partyers, but find ways to focus your celebrations on the coming of the Prince of Peace and the implications this

Def.: a logical relation btwn two propositions that fails to hold only if the first is true & the second is false

has for our lives both now and in eternity. At Christmas in particular we are called to be bringers of love, joy and hope to others. *These are the gifts*

First we need to establish and focus our celebrations on meaningful traditions that reflect our Christian faith and val-ues. Research your own family and cultural history and find out what observances your parents and grandparents grew up with. Look at your church denomination's traditions and think about ways that these could be incorporated into your observances. Research the rich liturgical traditions of the Orthodox, Catholic and Anglican traditions. These can provide tremendous inspiration for our own worship and celebration.

Latino families still enact the Christmas story as a community play called the Posada, which you may like to adapt for your family and other members of your church community. In the last week of Advent the figures of Joseph and Mary leave the parish crèche and move from house to house. Each family has the figures for a day and puts them in a special place with a candle burning nearby. At the end of the day the family brings the crèche figures to the next family another step in their journey back to the church on Christmas Eve.

Second, look for ways to transform the symbols of the consumer culture into expressions of faith. I suggested Robyn share the story of St Nicholas with her children. He lived in Turkey in the fourth century and was known for his expressions of love for God and neighbor. One story involves a poor man who didn't have enough money to provide dowries for his three daughters. As a result they were likely to become prostitutes. Nicholas walked past the house on three successive nights and each time threw in a bag of gold. He became a symbol of anonymous gift giving. Robyn encouraged her kids to focus their gift giving on those who were really in need and in so doing to remember the One who gave us the greatest gift of all – Christ our Savior. They volunteered to serve Christmas dinner at a local homeless shelter and bought a goat for a poor family in Ethiopia. "It was our most satisfying Christmas ever, "she said.

Making the Most of Advent & Christmas

Over the last few years I have hosted an annual blog series at
godspace.wordpress.com during the Advent and Christmas
season. Each year a rich feast of reflections are contributed
by bloggers across the globe who love God and love to share
their faith with others. This series has grown in popularity
as more people of all Christian traditions discover the value
of taking time in the days that lead up to Christmas to break
away from the consumer frenzy of our culture and prepare
their hearts and minds for the coming of Christ.

Jesus grew within Mary - yes, she was mightily blessed, but becoming the mother of God forever changed her life.

The reflections in *Waiting for the Light* are drawn from these
blog posts. They are designed to be used throughout Advent
and Christmas as both a preparation for and a celebration of
the birth of Christ. Each week of Advent focuses on a different theme:

> Week 1: Preparing
> Week 2: Seeking or expecting
> Week 3: Waiting
> Week 4: Becoming

The theme for the twelve days of Christmas is incarnation.

Each section of the book begins with a prayer or liturgy that
you might like to repeat each day as a way to focus on the
week's theme. As well as reading the daily devotions, I invite
you to join us in other activities that may help you and your
family focus more meaningfully on the Christmas season.
And don't forget to check out the additional resources and
reflections that will be added each day this year at godspace.
wordpress.com

Celebrate with an Advent Wreath

First I invite you to make an advent wreath. Set it up on your
dining room or kitchen table as a focal point for your celebration during both the Advent and Christmas season. An
advent wreath may have four or five candles depending on

whether you include the central Christ candle or not. We like to include the Christ candle because we love to light all five candles throughout the Christmas season. It is a rich feast of light during this dark season of the year.[1]

Take five minutes before or after your evening meal to light the appropriate candles, read scripture and the daily reflection included in this book. Consider reading the scriptures for the day from *The Book of Common Prayer*[2] as well as well as the scriptures we have highlighted. Each Sunday during Advent an additional candle is lit and then on Christmas Eve or Christmas Day, the central white candle is lit as well.

There are other ways to enrich this season of preparation and celebration too. You may like to set aside one evening a week – preferably Sunday when you light the new candle, as a family evening, to reflect on the events of the previous year. Alternatively go on a family prayer retreat to refocus your attention on God for the following year.

Ask each person in turn to answer the following questions:
- What is your most painful memory from the past year and how has it impacted your life?
- What are you most grateful for over the past year?
- What has been the most spiritually significant event in your life this past year?
- How have you grown spiritually in this last year?

Over the remaining weeks of Advent give each person an opportunity to share their memories. At the end of each evening have a time of thanksgiving and then offer the events that have been shared to God in a time of thanksgiving and healing prayer.

1. Instructions for making an Advent wreath can be downloaded from http://www.amazingmoms.com/htm/christmas_advent.htm.
2. Scriptures can be downloaded from http://www.crivoice.org/daily.html

Take a Christmas Eve Prayer Walk

One possible activity for Christmas Eve is a walk around your neighborhood with your family and friends. Imagine that you are Mary and Joseph looking for a place to stay until their baby is born. Pray for the people in the houses you pass that they will open their hearts and provide a place of welcome for the Christ child this Christmas. Pray the following prayer of blessing in front of each house.

> Lord, encircle this home with your presence
> Fill it with your peace
> Surround it with your love
> Protect it with your strength
> Lord, encircle this home
> Fill it with your joy
> Surround it with your hope
> Protect it with your grace
> Lord, encircle this home
> Fill it with hospitality to reach the lost
> Surround it with generosity to touch the poor
> Protect it with truth to guide all lives
> Lord, encircle this house with your presence

You may like to combine this prayer walk with a time of carol singing around the neighborhood. Or perhaps you could bake a batch of your favorite cookies to give to each of your neighbors and deliver them on Christmas Eve. Pause before you enter each house and pray for the people that live there. Or pray for each family while you are baking the cookies, enclose a special prayer with each plate. Here is a suggestion:

> God bless your household
> With love to surround you,
> With grace to uphold you,
> With life to sustain you.
> God bless you this year,
> Guide your paths to what is right,
> Your thoughts to what is true,
> Your minds to what is good.

Each day in every way,
May you be kept in the shadow of God's wings.

Christmas is Not a Day, It Is a Season

When December 26th arrives many of us feel let down because the day we have been anticipating for so long is over. The malls strip their elaborate decorations and junk their remaining Christmas stocks with huge 50-70% off sales. The Christmas wreaths and trees are thrown out for the garbage collectors and our frenzied activities give way to a low-grade depression.

Christmas isn't really over, however. In the sixth century it was decided that celebrating Christmas just for a day didn't provide time to celebrate all the joy that Christ's birth brought into the world. Christmas was made into a twelve day festival that ended with a feast on the Eve of Epiphany on January 5th to celebrate the coming of the wise men. In countries where this understanding of Christmas has not been co-opted by the commercialism of our society Christmas trees are not decorated until Christmas Eve and remain in the house sparkling with light and life until the Eve of Epiphany. This is the season during which we are meant to celebrate with joy and gratitude the wonder of a God whose love is so great that he sent his son to dwell amongst us. How incredible! How wonderful!

Sit down with your family the day after Christmas – read the story of the angels appearing to the shepherds in the fields. To me this is one of the most incredible stories in the Bible. Imagine it. Christ's birth even excited the angels. In fact they were so excited that they could not contain themselves. They had to break into the earthly realm with shouts of joy proclaiming that the promised Messiah had come to live amongst us.

Discuss your reactions to this story and to the whole account of the birth of Christ. When you read through the gospel account how do you feel? What is your earliest memory of when Christ first appeared to you? Share how you felt at that time and talk about the difference that Christ's presence has made in your life. Then ask yourselves: What most excites you today about the presence of Christ in your life? How does his presence impact your life? Next discuss ways that you could share the joy of Christmas with others during the following days. You might like to write down one suggestion for each of the 12 days of Christmas that could extend the joy of the season to others.

Here are some suggestions:
- Do you know people that are alone at this season? Take them out for a meal or invite them to go skiing or if you are in the southern hemisphere, swimming with you. Share with them your reasons for continuing to celebrate the joy of Christmas beyond December 25th.
- Do you know people who are disabled? Take them for a drive around your neighborhood to enjoy the Christmas lights.
- Do you have friends, acquaintances or family your rarely speak to? Phone one person each evening during Christmas to share your joy with them.

Entering fully into the seasons of Advent and Christmas enriches and anchors our faith. It may be too late this year to do much about your consumer extravaganza but it is still possible to take some small steps in the right direction and hopefully this devotional can help. Sit down with your family and friends and talk about what is really meaningful for you during the Christmas season. Develop a plan of action that enables you to enter into the joy of Christ's birth and the wonder of God coming into our world to dwell among us without the overwhelming pressures of consumerism.

Advent
Week One

Preparing

Liturgy for the First Week of Advent

The advent of the Lord is near.
New light dawning where there has been darkness.
The advent of the Lord is near.
New hope reigning where there has been death and despair.
The advent of the Lord is near.
New light, new hope, new life for all creation.

Pause for lighting of the Advent candle.

This is a season of preparation,
We prepare for Christ who broke the barriers between us and
God, each other and God's creation,
**We wait with repentant hearts to prepare the way of the
Lord,**
This is a season of watchfulness,
We watch for the One who heard our cries and shared the suf-
fering of our world,
**We wait in anticipation for God's light to penetrate the
darkness and shine within us,**
This is a season of promise,
We wait for the promised coming of Emmanuel, God with us,
God for us, God in us.
**We wait in hope for our Redeemer to bring God's love into
our broken world,**
This is a season of reflection,
We expect to be transformed so that we can serve in God's

kingdom as bearers of light.
We wait expectantly for God's Savior to come and dwell in our midst,
This is a season of fulfillment,
We await the promise of God's kingdom: wholeness, reconciliation and plenty for all.
We wait for God's covenant to be fulfilled, for God's kingdom to come in its fullness,
This is a season of joyful anticipation,
We anticipate the day when God's glory will be revealed to all people together.
We wait expectantly attentive to all the signs of Christ's coming.

Read scriptures for the day from the daily lectionary.

Lord whose light shines in the darkness,
Have mercy upon us,
Christ whose birth gives hope to all creation
Have mercy upon us,
Lord whose advent brings joy and love,
Grant us peace.

Our Father in heaven, may your name be honored. May your kingdom come soon. May your will be done here on earth, just as it is in heaven. Give us our food for today, and forgive us our sins, just as we have forgiven those who have sinned against us. And don't let us yield to temptation, but deliver us from the evil one.[3]

Into our troubles and weaknesses,
Into the barren places of our souls, Come Lord,
Come down, come in, come among us and make us whole.
Into the war torn and the refugee,
Into those who live in conflict, Come Lord,
Come down, come in, come among us and make us whole.
Into the homeless and the unemployed,
Into those who feel abandoned, Come Lord,

3. Lord's prayer from the New Living Translation.

Come down, come in, come among us and make us whole.
Into the sick and the disabled,
Into those with AIDS and cancer, Come, Lord
Come down, come in, come among us and make us whole.
Into the poor and the starving,
Into those who are oppressed or abused, Come Lord
Come down, come in, come among us and make us whole.
Into the lives of loved ones,
Into those from whom we are estranged, Come Lord,
Come down, come in, come among us and make us whole.
Into our joys and celebrations,
Into our work and our achievements, Come, Lord
Come down, come in, come among us and make us whole.

Pause for participants to offer specific prayers and thanksgivings to God.

Lord we long for your coming. Hasten the day when those who seek you in every nation will sit at you table. Hasten the day when suffering, pain, sickness, oppression and death will be overcome forever. Hasten the day when we will be resurrected as a multicultural family and live in peace, harmony, joy and love together in your kingdom.

Calm us to wait for the gift of Christ;
Cleanse us to prepare the way for Christ;
Teach us to contemplate the wonder of Christ;
Touch us to know the presence of Christ;
Anoint us to bear the life of Christ.[4]
Amen.

4. Ray Simpson, *Celtic Worship Through the Year* (London: Hodder & Stoughton, 1997) 19.

Advent Week One: Day 1

"Let the Season Work on Your Heart"
Thomas Turner

Scripture: Ecclesiastes 3:1

We are no strangers to time. We see it when our alarms go off, when the casserole is starting to burn in the oven, when we're late for work, when we're counting down days or when we watch them pass slowly by as we lie sick in bed.

We mark our important time by days, and our days by calendars and years, so that we don't lose track. We have school years, fiscal years, calendar years and election years. We have the seasons to tell us when to plant and harvest, and Memorial Day and Labor Day to tell us when our more artificial seasons start and end. Lost in all of this is what we gathered in faith communities for, what we should cherish the most: where is the church's calendar, the liturgical year, in all of this?

Luckily, Advent marks the beginning of the church's year, with a time of hopeful waiting before God. The Christian year, like our other years, brings order to our life, but instead of ordering when we have classes or when we need to vote, the Christian year orders how we are to be growing and living out our faith. The Christian year is a grand story, a great drama that unfolds year after year, continually calling us to live out the Gospel in our worship and our lives.

Advent is a season of meditation on the Messiah who has come and will come again. In Advent we journey with the people of God in our anticipation of the King who will come as Immanuel. In Advent we anticipate the day when time will be no more: when Christ returns to establish his eternal kingdom.

We would be wise to let this season work on our hearts. It is a season of hopeful waiting. It is not a season of celebration, parties, and splurging on gifts. Advent teaches us to reject this pattern of the world, the consumption and overblown materialism that is evident in our culture's infatuation with a Christmas that is not about a coming King but about the Almighty Dollar.

Christ spoke wisely when he said that we cannot serve both God and Money. During this season, let us turn from the materialistic striving and instead draw close to Christ. In drawing close to him, we identify with and proclaim God's narrative of love in a counter-cultural way, a way grounded in the Christian year.

Prayer: **Lord, during this Advent season help us to resist the instant gratification, materialism and gluttony that are the hallmarks of our culture's Christmas. May we instead meditate on how the coming of our Lord to this earth, and his anticipated return, call us to a deeply radical way of living.**

Thomas Turner is the Senior Editor & Publisher of GENERATE Magazine and an adjunct lecturer of English at Nyack College. He blogs at Everyday Liturgy. http://everydayliturgy.com/

Advent Week One: Day 2

"Pain Killers and Hope Killers"
Ryan Marsh

Scripture: Isaiah 2:4

Painkillers don't do what they say they are going to do. They might immediately mask the pain, but they don't kill the pain. They numb our sense of the pain, but they don't address the source of the pain. Now Iam not saying that there aren't good reasons to numb your pain. Sometimes there are...and it seems like Advent brings a lot of these reasons to light.

We read in Isaiah about a time when everyone comes running to God to teach them how to live, about a time when the world forgets how to fight, and a time when every tool to make war is re-purposed into a tool to make food. The drastic disparity between what God promises for the future and what we experience now is hard to bear. And Advent seems to highlight these differences. So it makes sense that during the season of Advent we encounter so much effort directed at pain-killing: excessive eating, excessive drinking, excessive shopping, excessive entertainment... The list goes on because our pain-killing strategies are as unique as our pain.

Karl Marx said that religion is the opiate of the masses. In other words, religion is the people's pain killer. And that is definitely one of the many shadow-sides of religion. But today Jesus is calling us out of our opiate stupor. Advent is the smelling salts of the masses. It wakes us up to all that is around us. It wakes us up to all that is within us, even if it hurts, because there is some pain that is linked directly to your hope and, if you kill that pain, you kill your hope.

This year, you'll know it's Advent if there is desire awakened in you today. You'll know it's Advent if you face the possibility of becoming horribly disappointed, but you risk hope anyway. You'll know it's Advent if you are beginning to feel the discomfort of reality and you recognize that you were meant for more. You always have the option of taking a pain-killer, but this year Advent is asking you to wait, confront your pain, and be shocked by the closeness of your God.

Prayer: **Lord, you ask us to walk towards you to discover the ways of life. May we enter this Advent season unafraid to confront our pain. May the desire for you awaken within us and give us hope.**

Ryan and his wife Bonnie inhabit Lynnwood, Washington with their precocious children Moses and Juniper. Ryan is the pastor of Church of the Beloved, a new church start that serves their surrounding neighborhoods through creative worship, intentional community, faith, arts and culture events, organic community gardening, and training entrepreneurial leaders. (BelovedsChurch.org)

Advent Week One: Day 3

"An Absurd Strategic Plan
for a Doomed Empire"
Tom Sine

Scripture: Matthew 6:33

The new empire God established through his Son was not
ushered in with pomp and circumstance. As you know, it
had its origins with a baby born in a cow stall in an undis-
tinguished village in the Roman Empire during the first
century AD. When Jesus began teaching, he announced the
astonishing news that his new empire had arrived. He made
clear that it would be unlike any empire the world had ever
seen. It came on a donkey's back. Its "imperial council" was
comprised of a handful of unemployed fishermen, a couple
of IRS agents, a prostitute and some other hangers-on. Jesus
demonstrated how to wield his imperial power by washing
feet, telling stories, and playing with kids. Jesus' empire is
based on the absurd values that the last should be first, losers
are winners, and the most influential in this empire should
clean the toilets.

Jesus insisted that those who are a part of his empire
shouldn't worry about finances, but simply trust God. The
resources to run this empire were basins, towels, and any
leftover lunches. This empire also developed a reputation for
constant partying. What was even more disturbing is that
they were almost always found to be partying with the wrong
kind of people.

Members of this empire are instructed to love their enemies,
forgive their friends, always give twice as much as people ask
of them, and never pursue power or position. Seriously, is
this any way to run an empire? Imagine what would happen
if you ran a political, economic or even religious institution
with these bizarre values. Clearly, it wouldn't have much of a
future. It might even get the leader assassinated.

During this season of Advent, how should we respond to the servant Jesus and his call to seek first God's Kingdom -- this absurdly designed empire -- in a world preoccupied with the pursuit of wealth, power, and position?

Prayer: **Lord Jesus Christ, you ask us to trust you in all areas of life. May we willingly lay down our preoccupations with wealth and power and respond to your call to seek God's kingdom above all else.**

Tom Sine is the author of numerous books, including The New Conspirators: Creating the Future One Mustard Seed at a Time from which this excerpt was taken (see p. 120). In addition to writing, Tom is a consultant on issues related to sustainability and spirituality. He is also the founder of Mustard Seed Associates.

Advent Week One: Day 4

"Reality Is Messy"
James Prescott

Scripture: John 3:17

Advent and Christmas are all about the coming of God, God making Himself present amongst us and taking human form, becoming incarnate, the act of God being willing to come to us to save us. But somehow, this idea can become romanticized in the midst of the flurry of activities and picturesque storytelling.

The reality? The story of the birth of Jesus is a story of an unmarried – though engaged – teenage girl who was pregnant; scandalous at the time, in any context. It's the story of a man who accepted her hand in marriage despite the scandal it would cause and the damage it would do to his whole family's reputation -- and potentially their income -- for a long time to come. And the story of a baby born either in a cave or in a dingy dark room hidden away, with animals for company, and laid in a food trough.

Not exactly the romantic story of Christmas we hear all the time.

But it's this that brings Jesus closer to us all – and makes Christmas worth celebrating.

This story tells us that Jesus is not just about blessing those who get it right all the time. He's not just about those who are favoured in the world's eyes. He's about the poor, the marginalised, the oppressed – serving, blessing, giving, loving and accepting all people for who they are, where they are, how they are. Through the story of His coming He connects with us in this. He empathizes with the reality that life isn't easy, that following God isn't easy and involves tough choices, and that far from being alone in those tough choices, He is right there with us, close to us, near to us.

By laying our lives down, by surrendering to God and putting Him first – as Mary and Joseph did – we can open ourselves up to see more of God this Advent / Christmas season.

And we can draw closer to God as we celebrate the time He came to us, immersing Himself totally in our human experience and choosing to experience life at its most raw and difficult.

That is truly a reason to celebrate!

Prayer: God, you entered human history a child in a stable. You showed us life in its fullness and experienced life at its most difficult. May we this season celebrate all you bring to us and draw closer to God.

James Prescott lives in Sutton, near London in the UK. He is part of Vineyard Church Sutton, a community trying to explore what church looks like in a post-modern context. He's currently working on a book on the Sabbath & God's rhythms for our lives, and his writing can be found at http://jamesprescott.co.uk/blog/

Advent Week One: Day 5

"Prepare the Way of the Lord"
Jeff Borden

Scripture: Malachi 3:1-4

"It is while waiting for the coming of the reign of God, Advent after Advent, that we come to realize that its coming depends on us. What we do will either hasten or slow, sharpen or dim our own commitment to do our part to bring it."(Joan Chittister in The Liturgical Year)

I consider how faithful I am to prepare the way for my Lord Jesus. I think, too often, we (generally) are lax, complacent, and downright lazy in our preparations. Where do we prepare…at some distant location, some time in the future? When do we prepare; hastily, at the last minute…out of desperation? Israel had (at the time of the prophet Malachi) 400 plus years to prepare…and they still weren't ready. Israel had (at the time of John the Baptist) several years…maybe even a decade or so; and they still weren't ready. Our nature indicates that our own preparation leaves much to be desired.

" the kingdom of God is w/in you" Jesus

I think "prepare the way" is repentance and with repentance we are open to receive the Spirit of the Lord to purify and cleanse us so we might receive His holy things. He is the giver of Light and our Guide in the dark. It is our responsibility to hasten His coming in our own lives through preparation…

So how do I prepare? I prepare with and through an attitude of repentance, with desire to walk upright in purity and righteousness. I want the sacrifice of my life to be a pleasing aroma in the nostrils of my God. Prepare. This word implies it is my responsibility to make the way ready for my King. He will cleanse, He will guide, He will purify… I am given the task to prepare.

Prayer: **Lord Jesus Chirst, as we wait once more to celebrate**

31

your coming, may we prepare our hearts in every way so that our lives can be a pleasing sacrifice to God.

Jeff Borden is an ordained elder in the Free Methodist Church of North America. He has been blogging and sharing his meditations since November of 2002 at www.icrucified.com/icruciblog.

Advent Week One: Day 6

"And I Thought My Sofa Was Advent Headquarters"
Kristin Tennant

Scripture: James 1:22

Yes, it's Advent, and once again I'm struck—frustratingly so—by the irony of a season that's all about peace, waiting, and togetherness wrapped up in a pace that doesn't actually allow for any of that. So I ask myself, what would it take to actually draw close to Jesus this Advent season?

Step 1: Locating Jesus

First, I need to find out where Jesus is. I believe he is "near," but where, exactly? (And for those of you thinking "He's everywhere!" yes, yes, I know, but that doesn't really help me calm down, stop running around, and focus.)

It seems to me that Jesus is in the simple, humble, modest places, where babies fuss and eventually sleep, where floors and windows are never perfectly clean, and where the only "decoration" might be a cluster of four candles and some evergreen branches.

It also seems to me that Jesus is wherever there are people who are most needy and vulnerable, who are feeling most alone and hopeless. He is near people who are waiting to be taken seriously—to be asked "What would make a difference?" and then to actually have their responses heard.

Step 2: Getting myself from here to there

I see those humble places, those vulnerable people, around me. If that's where Jesus is, how do I draw close? Well, for starters, I can go sit with a friend who has a new baby, lending support and maybe a bit of wisdom about strategies to calm the fussiness. And I can collect money from friends to purchase two baby swings for another mom I know with newborn twins. She has three other children, and her husband currently has to live in a town an hour away as he looks for work. She needs a lot of support and hope.

I'm not saying that my own family isn't important, or that having a Christmas tree up in my living room doesn't serve as a daily reminder that this season is different. But I'm also not going to fool myself into thinking that Advent is going to be all about cozy evenings by the tree with the people I love, knitting and sipping cocoa. There's probably going to be some busyness involved if I'm going to get myself from here to there—from my sofa and not-yet-decorated tree to the people Jesus is tending to. But I have a feeling that kind of activity will seed the very peace I'm looking for as Christmas draws near, and I finally learn how to draw close.

Prayer: **Lord, you come to us in the vulnerable and the marginalized. May we today slow down and take notice. May we draw close to you through the pain of strangers and respond to you in the needs of friends.**

Kristin Tennant is a freelance writer and author of the blog Halfway to Normal (http://www.halfwaytonormal.com/). She also blogs for Huffington Post, and has an essay in the recently-published Civitas Press book "Not Alone." She, her husband and their three daughters live, learn, play and worship in Urbana, Illinois.

Advent Week One: Day 7

"Live in Expectation"
Tara Malouf

Scripture: Luke 2:38

When a woman is pregnant we often refer to her as "expecting." Expecting…is that just a nice way of saying "growing outwardly large?" Indeed there is much expectation with pregnancy. We expect a baby to arrive and we expect cuddles and kisses; we expect little toes and fingers. But ask any woman who has been a mother for any length of time, and she will tell you that she has also entered into many things she did not expect.

To live in expectation and yet to be handed what you did not expect is what Advent is all about. The story of God in the scriptures is a mix of this strange dichotomy – expecting Him and yet being surprised by His ways. Often His people live with a strange mix of hope and bewilderment. They live in the reality of today's happenings and yet in the promises declared for the future. Even the idea of a coming Messiah was a deep, pregnant expectation; but when He arrived, there were many events and happenings those around Him did not understand.

Maybe expectation IS about growing outwardly large. It is making room for something that is about to happen and watching, listening for strange rumblings. It faces out and waits. Its opposite would be illusion, which turns us in upon ourselves, creating stories about what we think should happen. Illusion does not wait, but rather makes up what it thinks to be true. It doesn't face outward and expand u~ rather curls inward and causes us to shrink.

Advent is about getting rid of our illusion. expectation. It is about telling the familiar s desiring, growing, and birthing and also ent~

waiting for a Second Arrival. Advent is a time not only to read about Mary's pregnancy and the prophets' declarations, but also to expect the Spirit to birth something new in us. To live in Advent is to be enlarged, to feel the quickening for the Spirit's work, and to groan with the pains of labor. It is to shed illusion, live with unanswered questions and simply say with Mary... "Let it be done to me as You have said."

Prayer: God, we wait in expectation for your coming. May we make room for what is about to happen and expect your spirit to birth something new in our midst.

Tara Malouf makes her home in the Seattle area with her husband and two kids. She loves images and words, quiet and beauty, walking and prayer. She blogs at and shares her photography at http:// redthreadimages.com

Advent
Week Two

Seeking
or Expecting

Liturgy for the Second Week of Advent

Lord Jesus, you fill this place with the wonder of your love,
Christ who fills our seeking hearts show us your love.
We have come to you busy and you slow us down,
Christ who fills our seeking hearts slow us down.
We have come to you weary and you refresh us,
Christ who fills our seeking hearts refresh us.
We came to you searching and you renewed us with your life,
Christ who fills our seeking hearts renew us.

Pause for the lighting of the Advent candles

Speak to our hearts Lord Jesus,
In a language we can understand,
Speak to us, think within us, act though us,
Reveal in us your image.
Think within our minds Lord Jesus,
Teach us your rhythms of grace,
Speak to us, think within us, act though us,
Reveal in us your image.
Act through our labors Lord Jesus,
May we walk with you freely and lightly,
Speak to us, think within us, act though us,
Reveal in us your image.
In our work glorify you,
In our rest restore your presence,

Speak to us, think within us, act though us,
Reveal in us your image.
Through our study reveal you,
Through our prayer praise you,
Speak to us, think within us, act though us,
Reveal in us your image.
In our solitude make space for you,
In our community show oneness,
Speak to us, think within us, act though us,
Reveal in us your image.

Read the scriptures for the day from the daily lectionary

Glory to you Lord God almighty,
For the work of our hands and our times of rest,
For our times together and our times of solitude,
For our study of your word and our offering of prayers.
Glory and praise to Jesus for the sacrament of his life,
Let us give our work to him and so bear kingdom fruit,
Let us give our rest to him and bring forth peace,
Let us give our unity to him and build community.
Glory and praise to the spirit who fills all things,
May we be filled with the solitude that builds inner
strength,
May we pray with the wisdom that deepens intimacy,
May we act with the love that that speaks of God's king-
dom.
Glory and praise to God.

Lord's Prayer

God who created from nothing all that we see around us,
Enter the searching places of our hearts,
Search us, convict us, change us.
God who invites us to draw from the wellsprings of life,
Come into the dry and thirsty places of our lives,
Fill us, transform us, dwell within us.
God who extends to us the unforced rhythms of your grace,
Open within us a place where you can dwell,
Restore us, refresh us, renew us.
As we seek to move close to you during this Advent season,

May our searching hearts expand our understanding of you,
Live in us, love through us, glorify yourself.

Pause for participants to offer specific prayers and thanksgivings to God.

God today our hands have touched what you created in love and holiness,
Strengthen them that they may daily bring forth fruit to your glory.
God today our lips have sung your praise and our voices rejoiced in your sanctuary,
May the words of our mouths and the songs of our hearts glorify you forever.
God today we have relaxed together in the presence of your loving faithfulness,
Walk with us into the blessed hope of your eternal world of peace and abundance,
Grant that we who have tasted your living body and life giving blood may be renewed.
May we ever be restored and journey with you into the newness of life.[5]
Amen

5. Adapted from Liturgy Malabar.

Advent Week Two: Day 1

"Finding Jesus"
Julie Clawson

Scripture: Ephesians 4:22-24

It can be easy to despise Advent. I don't mean the period of waiting in hopeful expectation itself, but all the trappings of the season. It is easy to despise the commercialism to condemn the frenzy and the greed and see it as an obstacle to entering into a meaningful discipline of waiting.... From tacky decorations, to pushy sales clerks, to religious wars, the hustle and bustle and the secular trappings of the season often stand in the way of our hopeful anticipation of the Christ child. And so we despise it all, letting Advent become a time of spite and condemnation.

I've had to humbly realize that, all too often, I have let my animosity towards such things turn my experience of Advent into a twisted period of judgment instead of hope. And in standing in that judgment I have prevented myself from encountering Jesus in the very things I despised. I have found myself hoping to draw near to a Jesus of my own creation, a Jesus that liked the things I liked and ran in the same circles as I did.

But of course, my image of Jesus was a poor reflection of the real Jesus. Jesus was the one who was out there in the world, hanging out with the uncouth and common members of society. Sure, he delivered challenges to his culture and found moments for retreat, but he didn't shun it because he despised it for getting in the way of his contemplative spiritual journey. The Messiah showed up where no one expected him to. Born to a poor family in the unexpected dinginess of a stable, he subverted all cultural expectations.

If I desire to draw near to Christ this Advent, I need to let go of my judgment and condemnation of such places and be willing to see how Jesus appears unexpectedly -- even there. My narrow conception of Advent should not lead me to a place of bitterness and hate, but instead allow me to find hope in the redemption of all things, wherever it may be occurring.

Prayer: **Jesus, you so often appear where we least expect to see you. May our eyes and ears be open this Advent to welcome your coming in unexpected places and unanticipated ways.**

Julie Clawson is a mom, writer, and former pastor who lives in Austin, TX with her family. She is the author of Everyday Justice: the Global Impact of Our Daily Choices and blogs at julieclawson.com.

Advent Week Two: Day 2

"Along the Way"
Tracy Dickerson

Scripture: Luke 5:22-43

Awhile back, I received a tweet from Rick Warren (author of *Purpose Driven Life* and pastor of Saddleback Church) that said: "Study the STOPS of Jesus, not just his steps - the interruptions he allowed. Every healing was an interruption! R U flexible?"

Those one-hundred and forty (or less) characters prompted me to think again about a phrase in scripture that I love. If you look at the life of Jesus as depicted in the gospels, an often overlooked phrase crops up fairly frequently: Along the way. The Gospels are full of occasions in which Jesus and his followers stop on their way to their intended goal to do important life-affirming things.

We see an incredible example of this in Mark 5 where, on the way to heal a dying girl, Jesus first heals the Geresene demoniac (of we are Legion for we are many fame), and then he also heals a woman who had been hemorrhaging for twelve years. In fact, by the time he gets to his destination, the ill girl has died. Undaunted, Jesus resurrects her. This story reminds us in a profound way that the bus-stops and fellow sojourners that we meet along the way of life are as important as the destination. Through them, we learn the importance of being flexible enough to give these encounters the full attention they deserve. Finally, we see that everything always tends to pan out in the end, even if at first blush it appears that we have arrived too late to our destination.

With this in mind, as we wind our way through the Advent Season, may we make a special effort to be attuned to the ministrations of the Holy Spirit, and be ever alert for divine appointments as we seek to draw closer to Jesus. It is my prayer that we keep in mind that the re-discovering of the Christ-child is our ultimate goal but may we also be ever aware to the possibilities of finding Him in our interactions with the sojourners whom we encounter along the way."

Prayer: **Jesus, you often paused on the road to important destinations to minister to those you encountered. May we too, be willing to stop our hurried journeys to give full attention to the lost and abandoned ones we meet on the way.**

Tracy Dickerson is an Uber-churched/De-churched/Re-churched Follower of the Way of Jesus; She is the Wife of the Greatest Husband in the World, Mother to two awesome young men, Hospice Nurse, Seminarian, Church Planter, (and Plant Planter), Missional Thinker, Theologian Wanna-be, Lover of Parties, Celebrant of Life Abundant, Mover, Shaker, Occasional Sleeper-who is on a journey to charitably, graciously, healthily, knowledgeably live out the Missio Dei. Come and sit a spell with her at her blog www.nacreouskingdom.com.

Advent Week Two: Day 3

"The Least Likely"
Kathy Escobar

Scripture: Luke 9:48

One of my favorite parts of the Christmas story is how Jesus' arrival seems to surround a long string of "least likelies." God uses an average not-yet-married-so-it's-pretty-scandalous-to-all-of-a-sudden-turn-up-pregnant young girl to be the savior-of-the-world's mother. God's earthly father is a run of the mill carpenter. God sends angels to announce what's about to happen to some of the lowest-caste citizens – shepherds. God comes into the world not in a high-class hospital with the most skilled physicians but in a dirty, crowded, stinky stall.

Everything about the story is contrary to what was expected of the prophesied-about "messiah."

To me, that makes total sense. God's always been a little crazy that way – using the least likely to make a point. Yet, even though we nod our heads in agreement, we don't often integrate that point into the deeper places of our spirituality. I think it's because ingrained inside of humans is a desire for smoother, for easier, for strength, power, and upward mobility. It's like some weird magnetic force field always trying to pull us in to distract us. To turn our focus toward what the world says is important, valuable, worth-pursuing, toward "the most likely." The most likely to succeed, the most likely to work, the most likely to make us feel better.

So what am I looking for, hoping for, waiting for; what am I expecting – not just during Advent, but every day?

I want to see Jesus. I want to smell Jesus. I want to taste Jesus. I want to feel Jesus. I want to notice Jesus. In the flesh. In the spirit.

And I don't think I have to strive for it. That seems to be "the most likely" answer – that it's up to us, it's up to discipline, it's up to putting-our-nose-to-the-spiritual-grindstone.

No, the least likely place seems to be where I always find Jesus – in the sweet small ways my heart is pricked and I don't even know why, the beauty and power of a simple hug, a meal shared with friends, a kind gesture that brings dignity, one more day of sobriety for my brave friends, dollar store gifts that pass on hope. In gas money exchanged, in the dark places of friends' stories, in the flicker of a prayer candle, in the messiness of my house that often mirrors the messiness of my heart. In a long list of little ways that are so easy to miss if I'm focused on the most likely. These lovely small unlikely things give me hope.

And I am reminded yet again this Advent season that Jesus' unlikely entrance into the world, his unlikely mixing with the lowest-of-the-low and unlikely upside-down teachings don't just give me great hope. They also help me turn my eyes to the least likely, too.

Prayer: Jesu, your entered our world in such an unexpected way. May we notice you this Advent as you continue to appear in the least likely of ways, the least likely of people, and the least likely of places.

Kathy Escobar is a co-pastor at The Refuge, an eclectic faith community in north Denver, CO dedicated to those on the margins of life and faith. She's a mommy of 5; wife to Jose; a trained spiritual director; and author of Down We Go: Living Into the Wild Ways of Jesus. She blogs at www.kathyescobar.com.

Advent Week Two: Day 4

"A Flashmob Advent"
Barb Buckham

Scripture: Luke 2:8-11

One of the things that has delighted me this Advent is watching "flash mob" phenomena on Facebook and YouTube. They are happening everywhere around the world and in every setting; in shopping malls, outdoor plazas, grocery stores, a train station in Belgium, etc. I don't know who started this, but it's a great idea. I see in them a metaphor of the Kingdom of God. When you least expect it, when you're shopping, or buying a train ticket, or eating lunch in a food court, suddenly a song breaks out all around you with gifted singers performing the Messiah (my favorite) or some other fun song or dance. You can see the waves of delight and joy ripple over the crowds as they watch what's happening. Something is crashing into their busy rut and they stop and smile. Sometimes jaws drop. It reminds me that the Kingdom of God is really, really close. In fact it just might break out at any odd moment when we're chopping onions or sitting in traffic. It's that sense of anticipation that Advent brings. Come to think of it that was quite a "flash mob" when Jesus was born, with the chorus of angels in the sky and all.

I usually find it hard to "feel" close to Jesus when I have my quiet time. I struggle with my thoughts rambling off to something coming up in the day. But I do feel him come at odd moments when I least expect it. Something makes me feel alive and expectant because I know God is here, in a friend's smile, in planning a Christmas skit, in hearing a song on the radio, in making dinner for 25 on a relaxing day. And, like a flash mob, I really can't predict or control it.

I love Christmas and everything leading up to it. But I love more that Jesus is just out of the corner of my eye and at any time his Kingdom could break in and we could be dancing and singing and celebrating with him. That's one flash mob I want to be part of.

Prayer: **Jesus, your kingdom is close, breaking into our world in unexpected times and places. May we anticipate its coming and celebrate with dancing and song.**

Barb Buckham lives with her husband, Rich, in the Meadow Wood Cohousing community in Bremerton, WA. She currently is working on a variety of projects, including helping with a Christian movie being filmed in Port Gamble.

Advent Week Two: Day 5

"Entering into the Present"
Melanie Clark Pullen

Scripture: Psalms 139

I gave birth to a little boy a couple of months ago and went through a natural labour. My pains started in the middle of the night and continued on for ten hours, increasing in intensity and momentum. Every time a surge came upon me, I imagined myself scaling a mountain to its peak and then, as the pain subsided, I breathed deeply to relax and rest between the contractions. I didn't resist the pain, I tried not to tense up, I went with the rhythm of the labour. Eventually I entered what a friend calls that 'cathedral of pain' and delivered my son into the world.

The beauty of the experience is something that will stay with me forever, and I believe this is because I did not wish myself into the past of the pregnancy or the future of the birth. I managed to stay present, moment by moment. Sure, it hurt but I got through it and can look back on it with joy.

I'm taking that experience with me into Advent. It seems appropriate as I ponder Mary and her impending labour and the birth of the Christ child. Each day that draws us closer to Christmas, I set the intention to enter into the present moment. While the newspapers recount tales of fury and despondency, I share my daughter's excitement at discovering the wonders of hot chocolate and marshmallows. While friends talk about emigrating, I see a blueness in the sky that I hadn't realized was so beautiful. With my own future as a professional theatre and film maker in the balance, I breathe in the sweet, milky smell of my baby son's skin. And I am thankful, and I am content.

Because all we have is this moment, with all of its hope and pain, this moment where I AM exists, where Jesus is near.

Prayer: God, may we today cherish the whisper of each moment and wrap our hearts around your presence. May we make room to receive your gifts hidden in each minute and be content and thankful in all that it offers.

Melanie Clark Pullen is an actress and writer living in Ireland with her husband and two small children. She blogs at Perchance to Dream http://aislingdream.wordpress.com/where she explores spirituality and creativity.

Advent Week Two: Day 6

"Joy in the Glorious, the Ordinary, and the Dry: Part 1"
Idelette McVicker

Scripture: Psalms 28:7

My Advent journey is focused around a single word this year: Joy. Yep, I've said it, sung it, read it and celebrated it. But I have never inspected it closely, never allowed the meaning of joy to pierce me intimately. This word seems so ordinary and yet, as I have been sniffing it, swirling it, circling it and holding it close up to my ear, I am noticing its powers to transform ordinary moments into the holy, the sacred.

It's a word that invites Jesus close. In fact, I am noticing that Jesus likes to linger on the wings of my joy.

The quest started with a simple daily prayer I learned from a friend's kindergartener who learned it from her teacher: Lord, when did I bring You the most joy today?

I think about the question and this joy, this moment of deep happiness, fulfillment, awakening, gratitude, love around which the question evolves as I drive the minivan to and fro, to and fro, drop off, pick up. As I negotiate peace between a seven-year-old and a five-year-old before 7am. As I place laundry in the front-loader. Pick up the three-year-old's wood blocks and metal cars. As I sit on a small plastic stool to do homework. Wrap a piece of cold meat around a pickle and slip in a toothpick for a kindergartener's lunch.

Often joy seems distant, on faraway fields in different, quieter, seemingly more gratifying places.

The days speed by faster than I want them to. Many times I drive faster than I should. But this question a prayerful pause in my andante day reminds me that, just like now, Jesus was born into a big, noisy historical moment. Families and individuals rushed to the place of their birth to be counted. The census covered front pages, opinion pages and business pages. Hotels were full, streets bustling. Lives busy.

Who? A Saviour? A Messiah? Joy to the world? Yes, in the midst of the noise, there's a pause.

Prayer: **Come, Lord Jesus, come; fill us with you at your coming. Fill our minds with your words, our speeach with your thoughts, our hearts with your love. Turn us each day towards you.**

Idelette McVicker was born and raised in South Africa, which shaped a deep longing in her for justice, freedom and equality. She worked as a journalist in TaipeI before moving to Vancouver, Canada to marry Scott. She recently founded http://shelovesmaga-zine.com, blogs at http://idelette.com , writes regular contributions for http://ThoughtsaboutGod.com and tweets @idelette. But at the moment she spends most of her days driving, running and some-times dancing with her three children, aged 7, 5 and 3.

Advent Week Two: Day 7

"Joy in the Glorious, the Ordinary, and the Dry – Part 2"
Idelette McVicker

Scripture: Psalms 5:10-12

Heaven's own headlines pierced the noise and announced the day to those who were awake. Fireworks of heaven confirmed the birth. Angels sang Joy to the World on distant shepherd fields.

I learn: Joy is born into my ordinary day as I invite the Holy into possibly mundane moments. Joy to the world comes as I am ready, mindful, awake.

So I wake up before little feet scurry down for their first cup of milk. I sit and open up my heart and my life to the Word, to be birthed into these quiet, holy minutes. Into still, sane moments of the day when the rest of my house is asleep. I have to plan for it, prepare for it, set my alarm, wake up for it, fight for it.

Come, Lord Jesus, come.

Morning after morning, as I overcome my own slumbering body, Jesus sits with me. He wakes up the Life in me. I draw near. I sense the deep Joy. And Emmanuel, birthed into my ordinary human soul, sits oh so very close. Jesus smiles next to me. He rides on the waves of my deep joy. Already close.

But there are desert places in my heart, too. Grumpy places. Dusty places. Frantic places. Disappointed places. Failing places. Falling places. Broken places.

I remember: Come, Lord Jesus, come.

So I invite the Holy to the distant shepherd fields of my own

53

:s where my eyes are cold, not soft. In those very
; Advent, I am quietly beckoning, believing.

**:ome, Lord Jesus, come; into the mundane moments
of my ˻ay, into the failing, broken, disappointed places and
come close. Be birthed afresh in my soul.**

*Idelette McVicker was born and raised in South Africa, which
shaped a deep longing in her for justice, freedom and equality.
She worked as a journalist in Taipei before moving to Vancouver,
Canada to marry Scott. She recently founded http://shelovesmaga-
zine.com, blogs at http://idelette.com, writes regular contributions
for http://ThoughtsaboutGod.com and tweets @idelette. But at the
moment she spends most of her days driving, running and sometimes dancing with her three children, aged 7, 5 and 3.*

Advent
Week Three

Waiting

Liturgy for the Third Week of Advent

In this Advent season we await the coming of Christ
Come, Lord Jesus, come to us this night. We await your coming.
We await the coming of God's revealing light,
Come, Lord Jesus, come to us this night. We await your coming.
We await the coming of God's saving hope
Come, Lord Jesus, come to us this night. We await your coming.
We wait the coming of God's redeeming child
Come, Lord Jesus, come to us this night. We await your coming.

Pause for lighting of the Advent candles

We wait for the God of life
We wait for the Christ of love
We wait for the Spirit of truth
Come down, come in and dwell among us.
We wait in expectation of your coming
We wait in hope for your promises
We wait in joy for your salvation
Come down, come in and dwell among us.
Come into our hearts that we may love you
Come into our minds that we may know you
Come into our lives that we may serve you

Come down, come in and dwell among us.

Read the daily scriptures from the Book of Common Prayer

Child of promise, revealer of God, bringer of life come,
Come not as a distant emperor but as a helpless babe,
Come not as a prince in a palace, but as a displaced and frightened refugee
Come not as a man of power, but in love and compassion
We wait in joyful expectation.
Come to the beaten and the battered,
Come to the despised and rejected
Come to all in whom the divine image is still distorted.
We wait in hopeful anticipation,
Come to those outcast like shepherds in the field
Come to foreigners like Magi watching from afar
Come to rich and poor, young and old, male and female,
We wait with all the peoples of the earth
Come to bless all creation with your love,
Come to bring salvation on the earth,
Come to rule with justice and in peace,
Come, child of hope we welcome your coming

Our Father in heaven, reveal who you are. Set the world right; Do what's best—as above, so below. Keep us alive with three square meals. Keep us forgiven with you and forgiving others. Keep us safe from ourselves and the Devil. You're in charge! You can do anything you want! You're ablaze in beauty! Yes. Yes. Yes.[6]

Come, Lord Jesus, and lead the captives from their prisons,
Come, Lord Jesus, for in you we trust, O king of kings.
Come to bring peace in the midst of war,
Come, Lord Jesus, for in you we trust, O king of kings.
Come to offer comfort in the presence of mourning
Come, Lord Jesus, for in you we trust, O king of kings.
Come to provide abundance in the midst of hunger
Come, Lord Jesus, for in you we trust, O king of kings.

6. The Lord's prayer as it appears in *The Message*.

Come to show forth justice for those who have been oppressed
Come, Lord Jesus, for in you we trust, O king of kings.

Pause to offer specific prayers and thanksgivings.

Christ our Savior comes and we welcome his coming.
Not as a master but as a servant, not as a warrior but as a man
of peace.
May we put on the armor of light this night,
And clothe ourselves with Christ.
Put on hope to guide you, and love to surround you,
Put on joy to sustain you and peace to inspire you.
May we put on the armor of light this night,
And clothe ourselves with Christ.
We wait for the day of justice, and the dawn of righteousness,
We wait for the coming of light and for the advent of peace,
May we put on the armor of light this night,
And clothe ourselves with Christ.
Amen.

Advent Week Three: Day 1

"Active Waiting"
Kimberlee Conway Ireton

Scripture: Psalms 13:1

Advent is a season of waiting. We are waiting through the darkness of December for Christmas, but we're also waiting for Jesus to come again.

And let's face it, sometimes we get tired of waiting. Sometimes life is hard. Sometimes it hurts. Sometimes we cry with the Psalmist, "How long, O Lord?"

Advent honors this place of waiting. Advent invites us to embrace the waiting. Advent reminds us that God is present and active even when we feel like we're just marking time, or getting through, or barely holding on.

Henri Nouwen calls Advent waiting "active waiting." He writes, "Active waiting means to be present fully to the moment, in the conviction that something is happening where you are and that you want to be present to it. A waiting person is someone who is present to the moment, who believes that this moment is *the* moment."

I confess, I am not good at this sort of active waiting. I've spent most of my life thinking life was going to happen later, at some future date: when I got to college, say, or got a job or got married or had kids or my newborn twins start sleeping through the night.

But my life is right here, right now. Yes, I will keep waiting with eager longing for a good night's sleep. But I also am cognizant of God's mercies here, now: this gorgeous fall we've had, the many meals my church community has provided for us, a moment of silence in a house full of kids (a minor miracle, that!), a phone call from a friend when I thought I was at the end of my rope.

This Advent, as I wait through the darkness of December (and of sleep-deprivation), I choose to wait actively, to remember that darkness is not the end of the story. The Light is coming into the world. Jesus is drawing near. And as I wait for the Light to fully and finally come—for Jesus to fully and finally come—I will lift up my head, bowed as it is with weariness and worry, and look around and notice the places and ways that Light is even now breaking through the darkness.

Prayer: **God, may we today be mindful of you , remembering that each object, every act, all encounters are sacred to you. May we come to you in the wonder of this day and find eternal life.**

Kimberlee Conway Ireton is a freelance writer, mother of four, and author of The Circle of Seasons: Meeting God in the Church Year (InterVarsity Press). She blogs at http://www.kimberleeconwayireton.net/

Advent Week Three: Day 2

"Still Waiting"
Christina Whitehouse-Suggs

Scripture: 2 Peter 3:9

I do not like to wait.

Call me impatient (I am). Call me a product of the consumer generation (I am). Call me what you will...I do not like to wait. Which is why the season of Advent is so good for me.

I didn't grow up celebrating Advent. I'd never even heard of it until after graduating college...yes, think mid-20s. What a revelation! Spending almost an entire month preparing myself for the coming of Christ...instead of rushing into the season, thoughtless and mindless of the implications of the season for me as someone who professes to follow Christ (but rarely stops to think about what that really means).

And so, here I am, 10 years later, celebrating Advent yet again.

While many texts and sermons focus on the idea of "we are a people who are waiting in the darkness...waiting for the light of Christ," I have a different perspective. I believe this season of waiting is ripe with possibilities and full of hope and promise.

Seven years ago, I was seven months pregnant with Kara, my first child. There was fear and hope and mystery and a great sense of the unknown wrapped up in the experience. I couldn't peer into my womb to see her develop – I could only greet each new day with a sense of wonder and expectation, experiencing small flutters of life while waiting.

Yes, it was more tangible than our waiting for the coming of the Christ-child. Yes, it was a one-time event for me...not something I experience every year (thank God!).

But there is something to be learned in the waiting time. There is something inside all of us that is longing to be born – hope or joy or peace or love – every year! But it isn't something that can be rushed. We must nurture it, give it time and energy…and sometimes we must simply…wait.

Prayer: **Adventus Domini. Come, Lord Jesus. Come. We are your people and we are waiting.**

Christina Whitehouse-Suggs describes herself as a Baptimergent minister who is more comfortable among sinners than saints and still searching for her tribe. She blogs at Thoughts from the Journey. http://cwsuggs.blogspot.com/

Advent Week Three: Day 3

"Waiting without a Calendar"
Kristin Tennant

Scripture: 2 Corinthians 1:20

I love the feeling of anticipation. There are many things, big and small, that I anticipate, but nothing encompasses the feeling quite like Advent – that season when waiting is perfectly wrapped in anticipation, and presented as the best of gifts. Anticipation is what makes the waiting delicious and bearable.

As a child, following the well-worn path of rituals and traditions leading up to the candle-light Christmas Eve service, worked its magic on me. Several Decembers later, as a college student, I waited for that moment when my last final exam was handed in and I could hurry through the Michigan winter back to my dorm room, finish packing, and head home. One Advent years later, I was reading a book that described, week by week, exactly how the baby in my womb was forming.

Waiting. Anticipating. Counting down the days to a known end-point, a known result: Christmas will come. Exam week will end. This baby will be born.

Now, as I reflect on the idea of "waiting," it feels like a different creature – one void of anticipation. Sure, there are still specific moments I wait for with anticipation, like the family vacation we're planning for the summer. So much of my waiting, though, has become more complex. I wait for a sign, for a change of heart. I wait for inspiration and direction, for complete healing and reconciliation. I wait for the life I live each day to align with the life I envision in my head and crave in my soul.

In other words, the things I really find myself waiting for

can't be marked on the calendar. There aren't four candles to light, one each week, as I grow nearer to that point of arrival. The anticipation is stripped away, and I'm left with the waiting – periods of hope clouded by periods of doubt: Am I waiting for the right things? Am I hoping for too much? Will I even know when the waiting is over?

Yet that's exactly the kind of waiting we're actually doing, as Jesus-followers. I mean, it's important that we observe Advent as a journey toward December 25, the specific day we celebrate God becoming flesh and dwelling among us. It's important to teach our children that waiting can be active and so rewarding, and to demonstrate it with wreaths of candles and special calendars with small doors to open, gradually revealing the full picture.

But it's that full picture – the really big one – that we're actually waiting for. We're waiting for things on earth to be as they are in heaven, and we don't have a date on the calendar for that, any more than I have a date for when I'll stop feeling hurt about difficult things in my past.

It's true, sometimes it feels like the most futile of waiting games. Thankfully, we do have God's promises.
Those promises take what seems so abstract and uncertain in our waiting, and wrap it in the kind of anticipation we need to keep moving forward in hope.

Prayer: **Lord Christ, may we long for a world made new and a people transformed and move forward in hope and expectation towards your eternal purpose.**

Kristin Tennant is a freelance writer and author of the blog Halfway to Normal. She blogs for Huffington Post, and has an essay in the recently-published Civitas Press book "Not Alone." She, her husband and their three daughters live, learn, play and worship in Urbana, Illinois.

Advent Week Three: Day 4

"Holy Waiting"
Liz Dyer

Scripture: Luke 6:46-48

This Advent season it seems I am waiting for the same things I wait for all year – love, kindness, mercy, compassion, justice, and the joy and celebration that those things bring.

Sometimes I wait for it in myself as I struggle to forgive someone who has wronged me or someone I love…or when my caring seems to be turned back on myself and I am miserable because I am looking in the wrong direction…or when my humility slips away and I become a know-it-all defending my beliefs with prideful certainty.

Sometimes I wait for it in others as I watch innocent people suffer because of power and greed – as I hear hateful words spewed with careless abandon – as lives are lost due to war, disease, hunger, prejudice, disaster – as the oppressed, the disenfranchised, the outcasts are rejected or, worse, ignored.

Sometimes I wait for it in the church as I see exclusion, hatred, division, and apathy going unnoticed while some less significant issue seems to be at the forefront – as I see numbers and programs and rules matter more than individual people – as I see the church turning in on itself, protecting itself, nurturing itself.

Sometimes I wait for it in God – when my prayers seem to go unheard and unanswered – when I'm overwhelmed with all the injustice and suffering going on in the world – when it seems like the promise might not be kept after all.

Sometimes, I want to give up, to quit hoping, to quit believing, to quit waiting – but then I get some glimpse of the love that is being reborn, I see a flicker of the light that will someday be full blown ...

- In the man who leaves his successful, highly paid, glamorous job to start a charity for people who need clean drinking water.
- In the church that goes to a nearby neighborhood and does extreme home makeovers for those in need.
- In the small group of Christ followers who help those in need get their clothes washed and dried and call it Laundry Love.
- In the football team that lets a handicapped boy play during a real game and the boy makes a touchdown.
- In the mom (me) who learns lessons of love and grace from her gay son.
- In the God who became flesh and blood and moved into the neighborhood.

Yes, I wait all year, but the Advent season is a special time of waiting. It is a time to practice and train – a time to learn how to wait hopefully and joyfully – a time to be reminded of and reflect on the glimpses and the flickers of the past and the present – it is a time of Holy Waiting.

Prayer: **God, in this special season of waiting, may I glimpse the hope and joy of your coming knowing that there is nothing more precious than your love which is constantly being birthed in our midst.**

Liz Dyer blogs at Grace Rules.http://gracerules.wordpress.com/ She named her blog Grace Rules because, although she has a history of letting things like regulations, law, convictions, and stuff like that rule her life, she is determined to become a woman who is ruled by grace and love. She is married with two sons and lives in the Dallas/Ft. Worth area of Texas.

Advent Week Three: Day 5

"What Are We Waiting For?"
Ed Cyzewski

Scripture: Luke 24:13-31

What are we waiting for during Advent? In a sense we know; we read scripture, we pray, and we worship with our communities. We're looking for Jesus, and we want nothing more than to recognize his coming.

However, will we actually recognize the coming of Jesus, the form of God's salvation, or the arrival of God's Kingdom? Are we willing to go to the places where God's Kingdom is manifested, submit ourselves to the Lordship of Christ, and allow God to conform our dreams and desires to his plan?

When I read about John the Baptist and the many people in the audience of Jesus, I see a large number of people who eagerly waited for God and did everything possible to prepare for his coming, and still they missed it. They didn't recognize a Messiah who prayed in lonely places, worked on the margins, and challenged their preexisting lifestyles and religious practices. Even John had a hard time accepting Jesus after spending his whole life preparing to be the herald of the Messiah.

What are we waiting for during Advent? I'm not quite sure. None of us should be sure. We are indeed waiting for God to act, but we don't know what that action will look like.

Whether or not we recognize the fulfillment of God's hope and coming Kingdom will depend on our own humility and commitment to listening for the guidance of the Holy Spirit. Because, left to our own devices, we'd very likely miss out on the very things we've been waiting for.

Prayer: **God, we wait for you to act in unfamiliar ways and** unexpected places. May we sit quietly in the place where you draw close and know the intimacy of your sustaining touch.

Ed Cyzewski is the author of Coffeehouse Theology: Reflecting on God in Everyday Life. He blogs on theology at www.inamirrordimly.com and on writing at www.edcyz.com.

Advent Week Three: Day 6

"Awaiting the Morning"
Brad Culver

Scripture: John 11:1-7, 17-44

I love life. Every day is a gift. Each breath is a miracle. It astounds me to know the creator of everything seen and unseen thought to make food taste good and sex feel great. "L'Chaim, To Life."

Still, part of me groans, waiting to be delivered. Because, early on in the human story, a Leviathan of darkness entered God's world of wonder, pillaged the human heart, and left in its wake a trail of selfishness, despair, brokenness and oppression. As C.S. Lewis put it, "we are bent", desperately bent, crooked little folk in our crooked little world.... The moment we are born we are moving toward our physical death. We can't escape the fact that death is a constant companion -- but death is not the end.

Unless a seed fall in the ground and die…This is the rhythm until Christ returns.

Peter Marshall, the Scottish Presbyterian Minister who in later life was the Chaplin of the US Senate, used to share a story about a wee lad who, dying and afraid of the unknown, fearfully asks his mother 'What is it like to die?" She comforts him by explaining that death is like turning out the lights, going to sleep and awakening to a brand new day. On his death bed Peter Marshall turned to his wife Catherine and said, "See you in the morning."

I await the morning when I awake in His likeness. I await the dawning of a new day where death is no longer victorious, tears have ceased, sickness vanished, injustice, exploitation and oppression abolished, and we practice war no more. When finally, Empire gives way and "the kingdoms of this world become the Kingdoms of our Lord and His Christ and He will reign for ever and ever"…and we will wait no more.

Prayer: **God, we wait for your new world coming when the kingdoms of this world will indeed become the kingdoms of our Lord. We wait in hope for tears to cease and sickness to vanish, for injustice to be abolished and death to be overcome forever.**

Brad Culver is a mentor, teacher, and pioneer. He and his wife were a couple of bright-eyed hippy,high school sweethearts who have been inseperable for 36 years. They have 7 uniquely individual children, and 5 grandchildren who are presently the apples of their eye. They became followers Christ in 1973 during the Jesus movement. Their faith journey has taken them far and wide. Brad blogs at Living Water from an Ancient Well (http://livingwaterfromananancientwell. blogspot.com/).

Advent Week Three: Day 7

"Practice, Patience, and Perseverance"
Barb Buckman

Scripture: Hebrews 12:1-3

For several years I have had a growing desire to play the violin. This year, right at Advent, a violin teacher moved into our co-housing community. Then, I found a decent violin for a low price on Craig's list, just a few blocks from where I live. Bingo! I am SOOOOO going to do this. I am working on my second lesson now. OK, even the cat runs for cover when I practice. But every once in a while I play a single note that sounds beautiful. Yes, a single note. Then I hear a CD of an orchestra with the violins effortlessly ringing out a beautiful melody of a majestic symphony. And it makes me want to practice again.

As an adult learner, I know there are no short-cuts around practice, patience, and perseverance. I can speed up my learning with practice, but only so much. You cannot learn to play the violin in a week.

I've been thinking how much this is like Advent. We know Christ has come and will come again and restore all things. But in the mean-time, we must keep practicing our part with patience and perseverance. Whatever is given us to do we must do with all our heart. Our little stories are being woven into the grand story of the history of redemption. When the story is complete, the curtain will rise and the symphony will begin. We wouldn't want it to be too early any more than a pregnant woman wants her baby to be born too early. It must be just the right time. But as we wait, we practice our part. For our little part is important to the whole of the symphony.

Once in awhile we get to hear, or see, a glimpse of what we are waiting for – the breaking in of the Kingdom of God into this veil of tears. And it takes our breath away. AND HE

SHALL REIGN FOREVER AND EVER! Wow.

I'd better keep practicing my part.

Prayer: **Lord Jesus Christ, we long for the day when you wll restore all things. May we wait with patience and perserverance for the wonder and glory of your coming.**

Barb Buckham lives with her husband, Rich, in the Meadow Wood Cohousing, Community in Bremerton, WA . She currently is working on a variety of projects, including helping with a Christian movie being filmed in Port Gamble.

Advent
Week 4

Becoming

Liturgy for the Fourth Week of Advent

God we gather in this Advent season,
To hear the prayers you have placed in our hearts,
Filled with the ache of hurting people and a broken world,
We come willing to listen to the silence,
Longing to see and to become all you intend us to be.

Let the busyness of our bodies rest,
Let the worries of our minds rest,
Let the doubts of our hearts rest,
Letting go of self may we all hold onto God,
Opening ourselves to become a part of your new world that
is emerging.

Pause for the lighting of the Advent candles

God we release to you the rush and noise of life,
We breathe out all that hinders our becoming who you intend
us to be,
Fear, anxiety, busyness, confusion, guilt and tiredness,
We throw off our busy distractedness and breathe in all that is
of you,
Love, joy, peace, compassion, justice, grace and mercy.
God may we be mindful of you today,
Knowing that each moment of time is sanctified by your
spirit.

May your words echo deep within us,
So that we can hear your call to holiness, justice and compassion.
Becoming people of hope to a troubled world.

God may your silence penetrate deep inside,
Releasing for us the hope of this Advent season,
May it bring us to the place where love and justice meet,
Enabling us to surrender all that holds us captive,
Encouraging us to release all that has enslaved us.

O God as we wait to become your transformed people,
May we embrace your love and enter the place of deep communion with you,
Where time is stilled and place is fertile ground for seeds to sprout,
May we willingly walk into the unknown mystery of faith,
Seeking to become a part of your new world of justice and peace.

Read scriptures for the day from daily lectionary

God may we wait in patience and hope for what is emerging,
In our lives, in our world and through our faith,
May we be willing to walk on paths unknown,
That you have marked out with loving care.
May we wait in trust and not fear for your new world,
For the justice and peace and freedom that has been promised,
For those things hoped for and not yet seen.
Knowing that the future is in God's hands,
May we wait for the release and rest of your new world.

Eternal Spirit, Earth-Maker, Pain-bearer, Life-giver, source of all that is and that shall be, Father and Mother of us all. Loving God, in whom is heaven. The hallowing of your name echoes through the universe! The way of your justice be followed by the peoples of the earth! Your heavenly will be done by all created beings! Your commonwealth of peace and freedom sustain our hope and come on earth. With the

bread we need for today, feed us. In the hurts we absorb from one another, forgive us. In times of temptation and test, spare us. From the grip of all that is evil, free us. For you reign in the glory of the power that is love, now and forever. Amen.[7]

Pause to offer specific prayers and thanksgivings

God as we wait for your coming and meditate on your promises,
Grant that we may hear afresh the hope of your salvation,
And respond to the wonder of your forgiving love,
May we be filled with hope not just for ourselves,
But for a world in which all is made new.

**May we walk forward without fear into your ways Oh God,
And enter with assurance and trust into the love of Christ.
May we be filled with the hope and promise of the Spirit,
And greet with joy all the unexpected and unanticipated happenings,
That give us glimpses of what your new world is becoming.**

God grant that we may walk with humility into your grace and peace,
Our hearts filled with your love,
Our minds inspired by your truth,
Our wills strengthened by your hope.
Until at the end of our journey
We know the joy of our homecoming and the welcome of your embrace.

Amen.

7. Lord's prayer from the New Zealand Prayer Book.

Advent Week Four: Day 1

"God is Near; Draw Close"
Ryan Harrison

Scripture: Psalms 25:4-5

Everything I've done as this year draws to an end, I've done in preparation for a slow, peaceful advent season. It hasn't worked. I am distracted. My distractions are the brick and mortar kind, the kind that often have human faces (and so, human needs) attached to them. It is an avalanche of to-do lists, holiday parties, meetings, last-minute errands and urgent-need-your-attention-immediately situations that haven't stopped. And so, neither have I.

In past years, I would have been disappointed that my distractions kept me from experiencing this season, a time when I'm usually intentional about slowing down and experiencing God. This year, it's a different story. This year, I am decidedly attached to my distractions; they are safe and familiar. They dull the lacking, the missing, the emptiness that has rooted itself deep into my heart. They mask my world-weariness and my short-comings, my inability to love well.

They keep me far from God.

Accepting that God is near today, in this season of expectant waiting, would demand something of me that I lack the capacity to give. It would demand that I put away the distractions, that I step into God's presence and that I begin to hope. To hope that a different world is possible, that my work isn't in vain, that I won't always feel the lacking, the missing, the emptiness. To hope above all else that God's promise of redemption and restoration will continue to trickle down to me, until I see its fullness.

So, today, I'll lay down my distractions and I'll refocus on the One whose name is hope. I'll bundle up and walk in the quiet dawn, too early for distractions, while the cold chaps my face and reminds me of my pain. But the light will come, it will warm my face, and it will remind me to stop, to breathe, to pray.

Prayer: **God, may I today still my heart and lay aside my distractions, believing a new world is possible. May I focus on the one whose name is hope.**

Ryan Harrison lives in Denver, Colorado. Her days are filled with teaching, writing, and hopefully, especially in this season, spending time in God's presence.

Advent Week Four: Day 2

"A Cynic's Hope"
Ryan Marsh

Scripture: Luke 21:34

Hope. It wins elections. It fuels change.
Everybody wants hope. Right?
Sure. We want a hope we can wear on a t-shirt, but we sure as hell don't want the long dark night of hope, because hope is hard work and not for the faint of heart.
Hope ignites the painter's imagination when staring at a blank canvass.
Hope burns in the activist's bones until they tell the truth to powers that be.
Hope pushes the laboring pregnant woman past the pain to a child in her arms.
Hope drives the vigilant parent to wait up all night when a teenager breaks curfew.
Hope nudges the bored therapist into curiosity about who the person they sit across from is awkwardly becoming.
And hope is hard, hard work.
But most of what we like to call hope is merely a wish, a fantasy that successfully entertains us but for which we are unwilling to cry, sweat and bleed in order to see it come into existence. We swallow this kind of hollow hope like an Aspirin to numb our dissatisfaction with our present, but this daydream has little power to create actual change within us or anything else.

That's why, when we are honest about hope, we are, at best, rage-ingly ambivalent about it. We want it and we don't, because the wanting creates an aching void in us. And it's amazing all that we can fit into that void. The world's economy depends on it. Christmas depends on it! And it is our duty as citizens to have it, super-sized, half off, no interest for a year, right now. Yet in a strange turn of events, Christmas is the most hopeless of all holidays. The Church, it seems, is failing in hopefulness.

Fortunately, Christian hope is not wrapped up in the 'what', but in the 'who'. It's not based on a certainty around future events and timetables, or getting everything we want; instead Christian hope puts every last egg in the basket of this unreasonable trust that the birth of an illegitimate son of a teen mother in occupied Palestine is what God is doing to make all things new. That's a pretty tough hope to sell. So thank God that God keeps a promise, whether we hope for it or not. Thank God that God's kingdom comes, whether we pray for it or not. And maybe surprise will find us this Advent. Maybe God will put within us the strength to hope that Mary's son is actually mending the entire universe. That's something to be truly hopeful about!

Prayer: **Lord Jesus Christ our hope is in you. May we find within us the strength to hope that you really are mending the entire universe and making all things new.**

Ryan and his wife Bonnie inhabit Lynnwood, Washington with their precocious children Moses and Juniper. Ryan is the pastor of Church of the Beloved, BelovedsChurch.org a new church start that serves their surrounding neighborhoods through creative worship, intentional community, faith, arts and culture events, organic community gardening, and training entrepreneurial leaders.

Advent Week Four: Day 3

"Hope for Redemption"
J.R. Woodward

Scripture: Romans 15:13

What is the hope that you seek in your worship of God? The ultimate hope that is described by Paul earlier in Romans and alluded to here is the hope in the triune God's ability to bring about the promised new creation, the redemption of our bodies, and the redemption of the world. Instead of a world where creation is being polluted and destroyed because we act as though the resources we consume are infinite and the wastes we deposit are invisible, the creation, which is groaning to be released from the curse, will indeed be brought back to its original beauty.

Instead of a world where over 20,000 die daily of starvation or preventable diseases, it will be a place of abundance for all, because there will be a new relational economy, one that measures success in terms of gross national affection and global community.

Instead of a place where countries send their young men and women to war to fight others made in the image of God and spend billions a day to secure resources so that some can live extravagantly while others go without, it will be a world where nations will beat their swords into plowshares and their spears into pruning hooks. It will be a place, as the prophet Isaiah says, where nations will not take up sword against nation, nor will they train for war anymore. No more fighting, no more hatred.

Now *that* is something to hope for!

Prayer: **God of all life, may we hope today for a world in which abundance comes for all and resources are shared for the benefit of all. May we hope for a world with no more**

fighting or hatred. God may we be filled with your hope of a world made new.

JR Woodward is the co-founder of Kairos Los Angeles, a network of churches in the LA area He also co-founded the Ecclesia Network a relational network of missional churches and the Solis Foundation,which gives grants to help start small businesses among the poorest of the poor in Kenya. He is aslo author of "Creating a Missional Culture: Equipping the Church for the Sake of the World" with IVP due out Summer of 2012.

Advent Week Four: Day 4

"Being People of Welcome"
J.R. Woodward

Scripture: Romans 15:7

One biblical picture we have of the future is that people from every tongue, tribe, and nation will be living together with God at the center. As we read in the scripture above, Paul encourages us to be welcoming of others. We see this whole idea of welcoming in the Godhead, the very first community, where the spirit gives light to all people; where Christ gives his life for a world which is living in contradiction to the Father, and this giving of his life draws all those who believe in him into the eternal kind of life. We become welcomers when we remember the actions of the Father, Son and Spirit: the open arms of the Father receiving the prodigal, the out-stretched arms of Christ on the cross dying for the godless, and the spirit working in the hearts of God's people to accept those that at one time they had difficulty accepting.

An old Jewish joke tells the story of Judgment Day at the end of history. God summons all the people who have ever lived. "Here's what we are going to do," he explains. "Gabriel will read out the Ten Commandments, one by one. As he does, those who have broken them will have to depart into ever-lasting darkness." Commandment number one is read out and a number of people are led off. The same thing happens with each of the commandments until, having read eight of the ten, only a small crowd remains. God looks up to see this handful of stern, smug, grim-faced, self-righteous, joyless miseries staring back at him. He pauses and contemplates the prospect of spending eternity with this lot. "Alright!" he shouts. "Everybody can come back; I've changed my mind."

During the season of Advent, practice hospitality by joyfully welcoming the other in light of your hope in God.

Prayer: God may we express our hope for the future by extending hospitality towards others. May we joyfully welcome the other and walk into the light of your kingdom together.

JR Woodward is the co-founder of Kairos Los Angeles, a network of churches in the LA area. He also co-founded the Ecclesia Network a relational network of missional churches and the Solis Foundation, which gives grants to help start small businesses among the poorest of the poor in Kenya. He is aslo author of "Creating a Missional Culture: Equipping the Church for the Sake of the World" with IVP due out Summer of 2012.

Advent Week Four: Day 5

"Living between the Times: Part 1"
Tim Morey

Scripture: John 1:14

In Jesus' birth, the kingdom of God has broken into human history in a new and significant way. Yet the kingdom has not yet arrived in all its fullness, and won't be fully realized until Jesus returns. To paraphrase N. T. Wright, it's as if God has taken a page from the end of history and put it in the middle of the story. The glorious future that awaits us has begun now, and Jesus invites us to participate in the present reality of his kingdom.

Advent places us squarely in the middle of this reality. In this season we reflect on the first coming of Jesus, his virgin birth, God incarnate, the miracle of God Near Us. And at the same time we are reminded that the King will return in glory! So Advent reminds us that we live between these two events, the first and second Advent of Christ. We live between the times, in the already and not yet of God's kingdom. So how do we, as followers of Jesus, live out this reality? What does it look like to be faithful to living as Advent people? Let's begin with this:

First, we call on Jesus to help us live as whole people. God is restoring the world to the way it should be, and that includes restoring you and me to the way we should be. God's ultimate purpose for us is to fashion us into the likeness of Christ to bring healing to the places in us that are broken, to bring holiness to places that are sinful, to nurse to health the places that are wounded, to integrate us where we are fragmented. Advent reminds us that Jesus is making us whole, and invites us to lean into that work.

Prayer: **God, we believe you are resotring the world as it should be and renewing us to become the people we are**

meant to be. May we draw close to Jesus and allow him to perform the healing work that leads us towards wholeness.

Tim Morey is the founding and lead pastor of Life Covenant Church in Torrance, CA, the author of Embodying Our Faith (IVP), the husband of Samantha and the father of two little beauties, Abby and Hannah. He blogs at embodyingourfaith.com.

Advent Week Four: Day 6

"Living Between the Times: Part 2"
Tim Morey

Scripture: Isaiah 25:8-9

Yesterday we looked at the confusing reality of living in the already but not yet of God's kingdom. During Advent especially we wrestle with how we, as Jesus' followers, can live as faithful Advent people. We start by allowing God to fashion us into the likeness of Christ, to make us whole.

Here are two more ideas to consider:

We call on Jesus to help us live missionally. We pray with Jesus, "Your kingdom come, your will be done on earth as it is in heaven." To pray this is also to ask, God, how might you use me in answering this prayer? How does my presence (and your presence in me) in my home, my school, my workplace, my church, my city contribute to this world looking a bit more like heaven? We are reminded in Advent that God's chosen vehicle to bring about the reality of his kingdom is you and me, in the power of the Holy Spirit. Are we living missionally?

We call on Jesus to help us live expectantly. Christians are people of hope. No matter what today brings, a Tomorrow is coming when the King will return. Justice will come. Mercy will rule. Righteousness will reign. Peace will prevail. Tears will be wiped away, people separated by sin or by death will be reunited, night and all it implies will be gone, the sun itself will be superfluous in the overwhelming light that is Jesus. This year, Advent may find you in a place of joy or a place of struggle, but it reminds us all that Jesus will come again, that the baby in a manger is also the King of the universe, and that ultimately everything in this world will be as it should be. Come Lord Jesus . . .

Prayer: Our Father in heaven, hallowed by your name. Your kingdom come, your will be done, on earth as in heaven. Give us today our daily bread. Forgive us our sins, as we forgive those who sin against us. Lead us not into temptation, but deliver us from evil. For the kingdom, the power and the glory are yours. Now and forever. Amen.

Tim Morey is the founding and lead pastor of Life Covenant Church in Torrance, CA, the author of Embodying Our Faith (IVP), the husband of Samantha and the father of two little beauties, Abby and Hannah. He blogs at embodyingourfaith.com.

Advent Week Four: Day 7

"He Just Doesn't Fit"
Jason Clark

Scripture: John 14:23

On the day Solomon dedicated the temple he had built for God, he declared, 'Can it be that God will actually move into our neighborhood? Why, the cosmos itself isn't large enough to give you breathing room, let alone this Temple I've built.' (1 Kings 8:27). The absurdity that God could fit into the universe, let alone a temple, is immediately revealed.

Yet the Advent hope of Christmas is that God has located himself in relationship and proximity to us, such that (John 1:14) 'The Word became flesh and blood, and moved into the neighbourhood'.

If you are anything like me, I find that my life doesn't fit into my own life, let alone the creator of the universe moving in.

Here's the thing: too often we think of inviting Jesus into our lives, the Christian cliché of thinking that we open our lives and let Jesus in -- when we can remember to. The problem is that he just doesn't fit. Yet something entirely different seems to take place throughout the events leading up to Jesus' birth, as Jesus moves into the neighbourhood. He invites people into his life, and rather dramatically at that.

Mary and Joseph find their lives not just turned upside down by the arrival of a baby, but relocated around the agenda of the mission and identity of that baby. Shepherds struggling to make a living on the edge of society are thrust into the role of evangelists, telling others about the arrival of Jesus in their neighbourhood. And the Wise Men, powerful rulers and leaders, rather than have Jesus visit them, leave their positions of authority and travel to a stable in a foreign country to fit their lives around Jesus.

89

It seems that when Jesus moves into the neighbourhood, people have to fit into him. And maybe that's the solution to my problem today. I don't invite Jesus into my life;, he arrives to invite me into his life.

His life, as the new temple, is big enough for God, and for us.

So this Advent, I am going to stop waiting for Jesus to fit into my life, and instead ask and move to fit mine into his.

Prayer: Jesus may we no longer wait for you to fit into our lives but instead be willing to move, change and be transformed so that we are able to fit into your life.

Jason Clark planted an emerging church on the SW edge of London 14 years ago, while he was an investment broker in London. He is now a full time pastor/minister of the church, with a Doctor of Ministry. He teaches, trains and lectures on issues of church and culture, and is close to completion of a PhD in theology, that explores the affects of capitalism on church life.

Christmas Season

Incarnation

Christmas Liturgy

God of joy and celebration
God of love and mercy
God of peace and righteousness
We sing aloud and dance with the angels.
The ruler of all worlds, the shepherd of creation
Jesus Christ has come among us.
Our Savior Christ has come,
Not in power, not in might, but in the tenderness of love,
The promise of life hidden in a mother's womb.
In this season of God with us we celebrate with the angels
We are graced by the wonder of God's presence
We are filled with the tenderness of Christ's love.

Pause to light Advent and Christ candles

Love and faithfulness meet together,
Righteousness and peace kiss each other,
Faithfulness springs forth from the earth
Shout aloud Hallelujah! God's faithfulness comes down
from heaven,
God has kept his promise, the Savior has been born and a
new world begun.
This is the time we believe once more that perfect love casts
out fear,
That generosity transforms scarcity into abundance,
That righteousness overcomes oppression with justice.

Shout aloud Hallelujah! God's faithfulness comes down from heaven,
God has kept his promise, the Savior has been born and a new world begun.
We are graced by Christ's presence and filled with his love,
May we become bearers of God's light,
And go out to transform our troubled world.
Shout aloud Hallelujah! God's faithfulness comes down from heaven
God has kept his promise, the Savior has been born and a new world begun.

Read scriptures of the day from the daily lectionary

The whole earth shouts with joy to God,
The world declares God's praise.
Praise to the compassionate and gracious One,
Who sent the son to dwell among us.
Praise to the incarnate One, Jesus Christ our Redeemer,
Who fulfills God's covenant of love to all people.
Praise to the indwelling one, the Holy Spirit giver of life,
Who proclaims God's mercy and justice throughout the earth.
Praise to the three in One, the One in Three,
Praise to God on high.

Our Father who art in heaven hallowed be thy name. Thy kingdom come, thy will be done, on earth as it is in heaven. Give us this day our daily bread and forgive us our trespasses as we forgive those who trespass against us. Lead us not into temptation but deliver us from evil, for thine is the kingdom the power and the glory, for ever and ever. Amen.

Pause for a time of prayer and thanksgiving

Jesus you come,
In the voice of the poor,
In the hurting of the sick,
In the anguish of the oppressed.
Open our eyes that we may see you.
Jesus you come,

In the weakness of the vulnerable,
In the questions of the doubting,
In the fears of the dying.
Open our ears that we might hear you.
Jesus you come,
In the celebration of the saints,
In the generosity of the faithful,
In the compassion of the caring.
Open our hearts that we might embrace you.

Almighty God whose great love and compassion came into our world in the person of your incarnate son, Jesus Christ, plant in every heart your concern and care for all humankind. May the light of Christ ignite our hearts and shine out brightly from our lives, proclaiming your salvation to all the earth.

May the light of God shine on us,
May the love of Christ shine in us,
May the life of the Spirit shine through us.
This day and evermore,
Amen.

Christmas Season: Day 1

"A Journey of Longing: Part 1"
Tara Malouf

Scripture: Genesis 1

I stand on the edge of unformed worlds and watch them
come into being. I see light, brilliant color, and exquisite de-
tail. I hear rushing waters, animals calling to one another and
the sound of footsteps on the gravel. I hear the words "it is
VERY good" and those words are forever imprinted upon my
psyche. They churn in me images of intimacy with the Creator, my fellow bipeds and all creation. I taste joy and sweet
glory dripping off this newborn terrestrial ball.

Then tears…the sound of pitiful weeping and the thud of
an apple falling to the ground. The taste in my mouth turns
bitter with pride, shame, hiding, and toil. I feel the jolt of
a planet askew in its orbit. I must squint for the light has
dimmed, my eyes relegated to the spectrum of shadows. I feel
the stabbing pain of jealousy, murder, arrogance, love of self.
I am disoriented with the rest of the planet. I have become
"homo incurvatus in se ipsum" – man bent in on himself.
I am trapped and only a whisper of "it is good" lies below
audible frequencies in the regions of my heart.

I am hot and weary from wandering a planet that does not co-
operate with me. I hear promises and I hope; I trust…I long.
I celebrate moments of light when the "very good" seems to
well up almost to crescendo but then…always falls flat.

I walk, I lie, I settle down, I am oppressed, I am delivered, I
run back to tyrannical idols. I obey, I distrust, I watch gen-
erations die, I hope, I am faithful, I disobey. I watch leaders
rise and fall, I cry in agony, I am carted off to foreign lands,
I watch God be faithful, I am deafened by His silence. And I
wait…I long…for that "very good" rhythm.

I hear the sound of weeping again and this time find my face and hands wet with tears. I cry as a sojourner in a strange land. I hear the words of the prophets and they stir my soul awake with promises of justice, wholeness, and intonations of "very good". My tongue, so used to bitterness, perceives ever so slightly the taste of joy once again.

Then I hear nothing….

Heavy weighted under this unbearable nothingness lies my hope. It is suffocating – being executed by the crushing weight.

Yet in its final breath, a single Baby's cry rings out and shatters the grip of this oppressive foe. The weary planet shudders and takes, at long last, a gasp of fresh air. The Baby's cries reverberate to the outer edges of the universe and command the attention of a King – and the planet stands up straighter, a new creation process begun.

Prayer: **God we believe that in in the birth of Christ your new kingdom has come into being. May we look around and see where your new creation is emerging and join our hearts and lives to be a part of it.**

Tara Malouf is a photographer in Seattle Washington. One of her photographic goals at weddings, with family, or with children is to capture connections and relationships. She is also the producer of "The Story-formed Calendar," a unique calendar that revolves around the liturgical calendar. Visit her website at http://redthread-images.com

Christmas Season: Day 2

"A Journey of Longing - Part 2"
Tara Malouf

Scripture: Revelation 21: 1-7

For many, the Advent journey ends with the Baby's cries. The promised Savior has been born; our waiting is over. But I do not think it should end there. For we live in the unraveling story outside the pages of the Book – a story not so different from the one gone before. A story of longing and waiting and hope (see yesterday's reflection).

Though able to breathe, this planet still wheezes and coughs within its brokenness. It groans for full restoration – for the new creation to be complete. And I stand on its infected skin hearing children crying and people yelling. I feel the pain of wars and hate and cruelty. I, like back at the beginning, still taste the bitterness of sin. I still live with that awkward curvature of my soul.

And I wait…

Though I catch glimpses of Reality, I long for this Baby to return in the fullness of His Kingdom.
I long for Him to immerse a tired creation once again with the fullness of His glory.
I long for peace.
I long for a world put to right.
I long for the reign of a just King.
I long for healing and for joy to be the only flavor in our mouths.
I long for rest…for Shalom.
And I long to live fully in the dance of "it is VERY good."

Prayer: **Lord, as I wait for your Son to come again and to make his kingdom fully established, let me labor to make it a present reality – more visible, wherever I am.**

Tara Malouf is a photographer in Seattle Washington. One of her photographic goals at weddings, with family, or with children is to capture connections and relationships. She is also the producer of "The Story-formed Calendar", a unique calendar that revolves around the liturgical calendar.

Christmas Season: Day 3

"The Ugly Side of the Story"
Jamie Arpin-Ricci

Scripture: Matthew 2:1-18

The Christmas season stirs in us all kinds of sounds, images, and memories. For me, one of the longest held is the picture of Sunday-School kids in bathrobes with towels on their heads acting out the Christmas story. Yet one aspect of the story often gets glossed over: the massacre of the Jewish babies at Herod's command. Definitely not family friendly! We acknowledge it, but quickly move past it, for fear it might sully this otherwise joyous story.

And yet, Matthew's Gospel does not shy away from the gruesome story, which refuses to let us settle comfortably into the nostalgia of the season, confronting us with the brutality of humanity that accompanied the incarnation of God in the birth of Jesus Christ. As I consider the celebrations of the Jewish people to whom Jesus was born, I cannot help but notice how they have unwaveringly embraced the suffering and brokenness of their story as essential to their identity. Why then are we so quick to sanitize the story of the Advent of Christ?

Matthew knew that this story would stir in the hearts of his Jewish readers a memory of a similar story in their history: the birth of Moses. Just as the kingship of Jesus, proclaimed by the angels and validated by the Magi, threatened the powers that be, in the same way the Egyptians saw the growing strength of the Hebrew people as a threat to their control. And just as Moses rose up to lead his people out of captivity into the Promised Land, so too Jesus would rise up and lead all of creation out of the bondage of sin and death. Just as Moses gave up the privilege of his royal Egyptian upbringing, so too did Jesus condescend to take upon himself humanity for our salvation. And just as the story of Moses is hugely formative to the Old Testament identity of God's people, so too must we recognize these events at the birth of Christ as even more formative to our identity as his Church.

So while we must certainly celebrate the joyous season of Advent, we must learn to live in the tension that the coming of Christ was such a threat to the powers that be that it was inaugurated in the shed blood of innocent children. We must always temper our celebration with the mournful and cautious conviction that, as Christ truly incarnates through us -- his Body, his Church, we will pose an equal threat to the powers that be. And like Jesus, instead of seeking to sidle up to those powers to curry favour, we must follow Christ as he proclaims himself to the least of these: the poor, the simple and the broken. Through this foolish and weak community, the wise and the powerful will be confounded as his kingdom breaks forth in our hearts and in our lives.

Prayer: **Lord Jesus as we celebrate your birth as a fragile baby may we also remember that you were not afraid to embrace suffering and brokenness to lead all of creation out of the bondage of sin and death.**

Jamie Arpin-Ricci is an urban missionary, pastor, church planter and writer living in Winnipeg's inner city West End neighbourhood. He is planter & pastor of Little Flowers Community, in the inner city of Winnipeg. Jamie is also forming Chiara House, a new monastic community. He is a third order Franciscan with The Company of Jesus and is founding co-director of Youth With A Mission (YWAM) Urban Ministries Winnipeg with his wife Kim & son, Micah. He is the author of "The Cost of Community: Jesus, St. Francis & Life in the Kingdom (IVPress, 2011)

Christmas Season: Day 4

"Christmas Barbed and Barbarous"
Dave Perry

Scripture: Matthew 1:23

When juxtaposed with an image of barbed wire, the definition of the word barbarous is revealing. The vicious purpose of these short spikes of metal is to rip and tear flesh. Such wire is designed to keep out those individuals and groups deemed undesirable or dangerous. Those who are not like us. Particularly those who are foreign, strange, savage even. All across the globe, wire like this separates and defines humanity. It attempts to keep what we know safe and exclude what we fear.

The gospels take wire cutters to such barbed and barbarous thinking. Seen from the wrong side of the wire, Christmas is a divine protest movement that breaks into the easy enclaves and comfortable compounds of thought and behavior that deny others the right to fullness of life. And in Jesus, God leads the way, ripping up fences of hatred and distrust and moving right through to the vulnerabilities of the human heart, where love births togetherness and respect.

Christmas is truly shocking. And if the church domesticates the gospel and tries to keep it safe behind the barbed wire of cautious theology and timid mission, we will eventually discover just how foreign, strange and startling God is, when God cuts through and reaches us in all the raw, savage beauty of love in Jesus. Because the loving reality of God with us is barbed and barbarous to undemanding faith and harsh politics alike. The shocking truth revealed by St. Matthew tears down barriers and reveals God becoming real in the acute mess and muddle of life gone wrong. In Bethlehem hope for a world without wire is born.

And with bloodied hands and torn flesh, Jesus will show us

the true cost of such amazing love.

Prayer: **Lord Jesus Christ may we see in your birth the amazing love of a God whose desire is that all will be set free from injustice and oppression and hate. May we draw close to you so that together with all God's people we may share life in its fullness.**

Rev Dr David Perry is a Methodist Minister and Superintendent of the Hull (West) Circuit. Dave comes from the Black Country in the West Midlands. He has also worked as a research palaeoecologist. His hobbies include fell walking, rambling, running, reading, art, photography, model railways, red wine and watching CSI and movies on DVD. Dave is married to Sue, who is Deputy Head of Dietetics for the Hull and E. Yorkshire NHS Hospitals Trust. They have two daughters, Bekki and Judy.

Christmas Season: Day 5

"A Call to Relationship: Part 1"
Christine Sine

Scripture: Acts 2:42-47

Christianity is all about relationships. God created human-kind to live in relationship – with God, with each other and with God's good creation. Primarily the Fall broke relation-ship – it disconnected us from God, distorted our mutually caring relationships with each other and destroyed our stew-ardship of the earth.

We live in a world that still has a very distorted idea of relationships, and we often accept this without a murmur because our lives are a series of tasks to accomplish rather than a relationship-deepening experience. Our world majors on disposable relationships. We move, we change jobs, or we change churches and we disconnect from the relationships that under girded our previous life. Even our involvement in issues of social justice become tasks to accomplish that result in few if any relationships. No wonder we can swing from passionate concern about tsunamis in Samoa to child traffick-ing in Thailand without any concern for the impact of our swinging concerns.

And it is easy for us to justify our disconnect especially when our relationships are seen as tasks to accomplish rather than as opportunities to both experience and represent the God who cares so passionately for our world that he sent his son to live amongst us.

So how do we change our focus? First we must be willing to take time. The journey into intimacy in relationship begins not in busyness and doing but in quietness and solitude. Eugene Peterson expresses this beautifully in his book *Earth and Altar*:

The difference between privacy and solitude is profound. Privacy is our attempt to insulate the self from interference; solitude leaves the company of others for a time in order to listen to them more deeply, be aware of them, serve them.

Prayer: **Jesus as we celebrate this season of your birth may we take time. May we sit in quietness and solitude and drink in the silence that enables us to listen more carefully to you and to each other.**

Christine Sine speaks and writes about how to integrate spiritual rhythms into everyday life. She, her husband Tom and their golden retriever Bonnie love practicing hospitality and cooking food from all over the world. Her most recent book is To Garden with God Mustard Seed Associates 2010). She blogs at http://godspace. wordpress.com

Christmas Season: Day 6

"A Call to Relationship - Part 2"
Christine Sine

Scripture: Luke 5:16

In the scriptures we read often of Jesus withdrawing from the crowds, sometimes with his disciples but often alone, to pray. As we consider yesterday's quote from Eugene Peterson, it seems we find another of the great paradoxes of God: developing deeper relationships does not begin with more time spent with people but with more time spent in solitude with God. It doesn't begin with getting out into the crowds and the multitudes but with drawing aside into a quiet place to pray. And in that quiet place prayer is not about us doing something before God, it is about listening. It is not about prayers that express our concern for the world, it is about opening up the doors and the windows of our souls to the presence of a God who is never more than a breath away. It is about allowing God to fill every fiber of our being so that all that we are and do flows out of a deeply rooted relationship with the God of all creation.

No wonder Jesus could be so attentive to the crowds that followed him. No wonder he had such wisdom and insights into the behavior of his disciples. No wonder he had such confidence in what God was and wasn't asking him to do. His life was lived amongst the crowds but was grounded in solitude. His kingdom-building work of healing, releasing the oppressed, and preaching the good news to the poor flowed out of a confident and intimate relationship with God, not out of a need to respond to the demands of the broken world around him.

As we begin a new year, this would be a great time to get away for retreat and quiet. It is an essential time to focus on deepening our relationship with God in solitude and reflection, so that we can be better equipped to move out into the world as God's hearts and hands.

Prayer: **God may we listen to you in the silence of solitude, knowing that it is in this set apart place and set apart time that we are best equipped to go out into the world as your hands of compassion and hearts of love.**

Christine Sine speaks and writes about how to integrate spiritual rhythms into everyday life. She, her husband Tom and their golden retriever Bonnie love practicing hospitality and cooking food from all over the world. Her most recent book is To Garden with God Mustard Seed Associates 2010). She blogs at http://godspace. wordpress.com.

Christmas Season: Day 7

"Making Room for the Unexpected"
Kathy Escobar

Scripture: Zechariah 4:10

We can get so stuck in the patterns of our day to day that we can miss out on small little God interruptions that I call "God interference." To me, God interference are moments where God is trying to get our attention in some small or big way to help break the cycle of our busyness, in-grown eyeballs, or being a victim of our circumstances. In Christ-is-born stories in the gospels, I am reminded of how God interfered and interrupted Mary and Elizabeth's lives with baby boys they never expected. They responded to these huge, scary inter-ruptions with joy and faith. I wonder what we are doing with the smaller ones in our own lives?

One of my favorite parts of the Jesus story is just how "unex-pected" he really was. They were hoping for a strong-power-ful-in-the-world's-eyes messiah. Instead, they got a humble servant born as a baby to an unlikely couple in a stinky manger. What the world says Christmas is about is not what Christmas is about.

Jesus came in an unexpected way – and He seems still to show up in unexpected contrary-to-the-world ways. In pov-erty. In sickness. In desperation. In darkness. In the trenches of people's real lives.

And so even though Advent is a time of expectation, I won-der if we need to make more room for the unexpected. To be open to small or big slivers of light & love & peace & joy in places we're not used to seeing them.

Yes, this year I really want to be open to hope in unexpected places.

Prayer: **God-of-the-unexpected, may we make room for your movement in our lives, in our relationships, in our neighborhoods, in our cities, in our world. May we hope for your appearing in all the unexpected places of our lives.**

Kathy Escobar is a co-pastor at The Refuge, an eclectic faith community in north Denver, CO dedicated to those on the margins of life and faith. She's a mommy of 5; wife to Jose; a trained spiritual director; and author of Down We Go: Living Into the Wild Ways of Jesus. She blogs at www.kathyescobar.com.

Christmas Season: Day 8

"A Lesson from Mary"
Jude Tiersma Watson

Scripture: Luke 1:46-55

Before moving into central Los Angeles 20 years ago, I had not thought that much about Mary. Mary was in the domain of my Catholic friends; we Protestants did not spend much time with her. But in my Latino immigrant neighborhood, Mary was everywhere, especially the Mexican incarnation known as the Virgin of Guadalupe. Her image was painted on every corner. As I got to know the girls and young women in my building, they often would ask me, knowing I was not Catholic, Do you believe in Mary? After some reflection, I responded, Yes, I believe in Mary. Let's see what the Bible says about Mary."

Thus I discovered Mary with my young friends, as we read Luke 1 and 2 together. I heard more deeply the wonder, the surrender, the ruthless trust in Mary's words, "Here am I, the servant of the Lord. Let it be with me according to your word." I wondered what it would have been like to be Mary. Could she have known, at her young age, what it would all mean? What lay before her?

As the months passed, I would come to identify more intimately with Mary, the mother who treasured and pondered so much in her heart, and whose own heart would be pierced. As my neighbors became my friends, as they trusted me with the stories of their lives, I too treasured and guarded many things in my heart. As we have walked together through the joys but also deep sorrow and struggle in their lives, my heart too has been pierced.

But Mary's song, the Magnificat, gives perspective and reminds us that this is not the end of the story. Mary's trust is in God, in the fulfillment of the promise made to her ancestors.

In the Magnificat, we see where her joy lies: "My soul magnifies the Lord, and my spirit rejoices in God my Savior".

We see in Mary that Christmas joy is not separate from the struggles of life, but breaks through the struggles, just as Jesus, the Light of the World, broke into our world when he was born to Mary that very first Christmas.

Prayer: **May we walk through this Christmas season cherishing the special hopes that God has placed in our hearts. May we share Mary's joy at the birth of a son born to be savior of the world yet not be afraid to embrace Mary's pain recognizing that all hope is interwoven with the struggles of life.**

Jude Tiersma Watson is Associate Professor of Urban Mission at Fuller Seminary in Pasadena. She has lived for 20 years in an immigrant neighborhood as a member of InnerChange, a Christian Order Among the Poor.

Christmas Season: Day 9

"The Stone Child"
Shawn Small

Scripture: John 1: 1-18

I push through the bustling streets of London to Trafalgar Square toward the Church of St-Martin-in-the-Field. I have come to gather information on concerts, but as I climb the steps that lead up to the sanctuary, I am halted by an unusual stone sculpture that dominates the middle of the large covered entrance. A hewn block of granite stands almost at eye level. Bare in its form, and cold to the touch, the four smooth sides have a simple inscription that wraps around the top of the obelisk: "IN THE BEGINNING THERE WAS THE WORD. THE WORD BECAME HUMAN & LIVED AMONG US." St. John 1:1, 14.

Unlike its sides, the top of the obelisk is rough and pockmarked, like a lake suddenly barraged by a violent rainstorm. Out of the middle of that stone, as if pushed through the rock into the world, rises the newborn God-Child. His eyes are still closed as he emerges out of his mother's womb. He is naked, exposed to the elements, still attached to the umbilical cord that winds back into the rock.

It is the beautiful disturbing mystery, captured within this memorial, that unexpectedly holds me bound between two worlds for these few minutes. The idea of the Incarnation, God come to earth wrapped in human flesh, both comforts and confounds me. Yet, without this mystery we have an untouchable, invisible God. Literal incarnation separates Christ from humanity's great labyrinth of gods. To have a God who wrestled in the mud of humanity, who experienced pain and loss, who I can never say, "You don't understand" to; that is a God who seeks me. The transcendence I toil and trouble over starts with His incarnation. He has broken through creation, into the world of his making. The Author has entered the

111

story as the central character, but in doing so, he has decided to follow by our rules.

This baby, pushed through the granite, is vulnerable and in need of the protection and sustenance of others. Vulnerable omniscience, vulnerable omnipotence, vulnerable omnipresence; my head spins while my heart flies.

I walk away, on to my tasks, remembering the Word became flesh. A child of stone was sent to soften the stony hearts of humanity. My stony heart just softened a bit more.

Prayer: **God you have come into our world as a child, vulnerable yet omnipotent, God become human. Incomprehensible, unbelieveable. May we too stop in awe at your emerging and allow you to soften our stony hearts.**

Shawn Small is the author of The Via Advent, a delightful book that chronicles the story of Jesus birth in story form. Shawn blogs at Occasionally Musing at http://shawnsmallstories.com

Christmas Season: Day 10

"Let Our Eyes Be Opened"
Kimberlee Conway Ireton

Scripture: Matthew 20:32-34

In the midst of my days, I cry out with the blind men, "Lord Jesus Christ, Son of God, have mercy on me!" I pray that a lot, the Jesus Prayer. Often it's my response to Jesus' question, What do you want? I want mercy, Lord, and help. But the blind men start there, and end with, We want to see. Let our eyes be opened.

Let our eyes be opened.

It's a good prayer, and a wise one. Also—dangerous. I think we do not always want to see. But I want to want sight. I want to want to see. And so this, too, is my prayer.
Let my eyes be opened to You, present and playing and working and praying in me and with me and beside me.

Let my eyes be opened to the way You shine through others, and to You when You are hidden in them, Your image all but erased, blotted out by anger or despair or bitterness or hopelessness.

Let my eyes be opened to the wonder of Your world, to the marvel of steely seas under gray skies; to the beauty of red rosehips on yellowing hedgeroses beneath the bare branches of vine maples and deep green cedars; to the sound of geese flying low over a marsh and settling in a field at its edges, their honking loud and joyful, the beating of their wings stirring the air as they rise and fly again.

Let my eyes be opened to You, Jesus, God incarnate, God-made-flesh, Emmanuel, God-with-us…God-in-us.

Let my eyes be opened to You in me, Your still small voice

prompting me, Your strength enabling me to be patient when I feel frantic, to keep silent when I want to scream in frustration, to touch gently when I want to grab or shove, to show love even when I feel anything but loving.

Let my eyes be opened.

Let my eyes be opened that I may regain my sight and follow where You lead.

Prayer: God let our eyes be opened. May we see you in the face of others, in the wonders of creation, in the beauty of our world. Jesus, God-incarnate, God-made-flesh, Emmanuel, God with us, God in us let our eyes be opened to you.

Kimberlee Conway Ireton is the author of The Circle of Seasons: Meeting God in the Church Year. You can visit her online at http:// kimberleeconwayireton.net.

Christmas Season: Day 11

"Did You Get What You Expected?"
Christine Sine

Scripture: Matthew 2:13-18

Christmas Day has come and gone. Even the after-Christmas sales, far more exciting for some than the birth of Christ, are now well behind us. But did any of us really get what we expected? This season, long anticipated by many of us as the celebration of the birth of Christ our Savior, often comes with unexpected consequences. The gifts never quite meet everyone's expectations and leave behind mountains of wrapping paper and ribbon that will add yet more indestructible rubbish to the landfills.

The birth of Christ wasn't quite what was expected either. Two thousand years ago he appeared in an unexpected place and in an unexpected way. His birth was ignored by the religious leaders who were looking for a king to increase their privilege and power. It threatened the political leaders who retaliated by vengefully killing all infants around Bethlehem. I am not sure that those who encountered the baby Jesus found what they expected either. The Magi after their long and arduous journey must have expected far more than an ordinary looking infant born to a young inexperienced mother. And the shepherds who experienced the incredible spectacle of angels singing in the heavens must have come looking for someone quite extraordinary.

Today too we often find in Jesus what we least expect. Maybe we have come looking for a child born in a stable, an unassuming infant whose advent makes us feel good but does not impose difficult demands. Instead we have found a revolutionary leader whose words and actions turned the world upside down.

Babies born in the backwater of civilization are easy to ignore.

115

Yet even a child disrupts the world of its parents and makes demands that turn their world upside down. So it is with Jesus. We welcome him as a cute little baby but if we continue to journey with him, we soon realize that he wants to turn our world upside down. That cute little baby in the manger scene has indeed become a revolutionary leader who is slowly transforming everything we are and do.

Prayer: Jesus you have come into our world but not as we expected. May we we open our eyes to see you, not as a child in a manger but as that revolutionary leader who is slowly transforming everything we are and do.

Christine Sine speaks and writes about how to integrate spiritual rhythms into everyday life. She, her husband Tom and their golden retriever Bonnie love practicing hospitality and cooking food from all over the world. Her most recent book is To Garden with God Mustard Seed Associates 2010). She blogs at http://godspace. wordpress.com

Christmas Season: Day 12

"The Eve of Epiphany"
Christine Sine

Scripture: Matthew 2:1-12

January 5th, the Eve of Epiphany, marks the end of the Christmas season and ushers in the season of epiphany. The dictionary defines "epiphany" as a "revealing, a manifestation, an unveiling." In the coming season we will celebrate the revealing of Jesus as God and the fact that Christ's lordship over all creation is revealed, made manifest and unveiled.

There are three events often associated with Epiphany. Jesus is revealed as Son of God to the Magi, travelers from distant lands who come to worship and give this king their tribute, showing Jesus' epiphany as Son of God reaches to the ends of the earth. Second, Jesus is revealed to John the Baptist, his disciples and the repentant crowds by the Jordan river, showing what is necessary to make Israel ready for the Messiah's coming. Third, Jesus is revealed as Son of God to the wedding guests at Cana as he performs his first miracle and turns water into wine. Here he unveils our first glimpse of a new kingdom of celebration and joy, a kingdom in which the hungry are fed, the sick are healed, the oppressed are set free, justice comes for the poor and good news is preached to all creation.

This final celebration of the Christmas season is therefore also an invitation. Jesus' coming as Son of God reaches across time and space beckoning us to embrace God's call to come and see, come and follow, go and tell others. We are invited to walk into the coming days not only filled with but also sharing the love that has been so generously lavished on us through the birth of Christ. Because Christ is present among us as a messenger of hope for all peoples, we must respond to his call to reveal him to others so that they too may know him as Son of God and experience the hope his message brings.

Take Action

There are many ways that you could reveal the message of hope to others during the season of Epiphany. As the Christmas season draws to a close with one final celebration on the Eve of Epiphany take time to consider how you may reveal Christ to others during the coming weeks.

Consider doing one of the following during the weeks of Epiphany

1. Do you have new neighbors? Are there newcomers to your church? Invite them over for an evening to get better acquainted

2. Is this an opportunity to reach out to people in your office or workplace? Consider providing breakfast for those you work with. If you are feeling particularly adventurous you might like to make this a weekly or monthly event.

3. Is there a university close by with international students? Invite a small group of students home for lunch or dinner. This is a great way to get know about another culture and the students will be very eager to learn more about your culture and religious traditions.

4. Is there a senior care facility near where you live? Take your children over for a visit. Get them to read a story or sing a song for the residents. Consider taking some of the elderly people out for a trip.

5. Is there a special way in which your children could reach out to others at their school or play group? Talk to them about the Biblical story and ask them to come up with one way that they could reveal the hope of God the their playmates.

Prayer for Eve of Epiphany

Arise, shine inheritors of God's light,
Bearers of Christ's light to our darkened world,
The light of God has come into our world,
And nations will come to its brightness,
Arise, shine, privileged ones who live in the light of Christ,
Bow before God not in shame but in awe,
All is visible in Christ's eternal light,
In us God's light never goes out.
Arise shine, in Christ, God's light has been revealed to us,
It reaches across time and space,
We have come to see,
We have come to follow,
Arise shine, in Christ God's light has been revealed to all
people,
God's glory has been unveiled in all the earth,
May we go and tell,
May we go and share God's light with our needy world.

Pause to light Advent and Christmas candles

Come and see
The light of God has come into our world
To proclaim God's justice and love
It has overcome the darkness and brought new life
Come and follow
Christ our king has redeemed our world
He draws us into a loving family
From every tribe and nation and culture
Go and tell
The Spirit has equipped us for service
To love our neighbors as we do ourselves
To bring God's salvation to the ends of the earth
Come and see, come and follow, go and tell
In God's Son the nations of the earth will put their hope

Read Scriptures of the day from Daily Lectionary

God we have come to see and we will follow and show others,
In times of scarcity we will see your generosity,
In places of oppression we will see your freedom,
In a world at war we will see your peace.
God we have come to see and we will follow and show others,
In times of despair we will follow your hope,
In places of hate we will follow your love,
In a world of deception we will follow your truth.
God we have come to see and we will follow and show others,
In times of uncertainty we will show your faithfulness,
In places of corruption we will show your righteousness,
In a world of bondage will we show your salvation.

Our Father who art in heaven, hallowed be your name,
Your kingdom come, your will be done, on earth as it is in
heaven. Give us this day our daily bread, and forgive us our
trespasses as we forgive those who trespass against us. And
lead us not into temptation, but deliver us from evil, for
yours is the kingdom, the power and the glory, forever and
ever. Amen.

God who revealed yourself to wise men following a star,
Guide all who search and journey towards your light today,
God whose light shines like a bright guiding star have
mercy on us.
God who unveiled yourself in the gift of a son,
Show yourself to all who seek after justice and righteousness
today,
God whose light shines like a bright guiding star have
mercy on us.
God who was baptized with those who declared their repentance in the Jordan river,
Manifest yourself to all who come with repentant hearts
today,
God whose light shines like a bright guiding star have
mercy on us.
God who fed the five thousand with a handful of fish and
loaves,

Satisfy our hunger with your word of truth and love,
God whose light shines like a bright guiding star have mercy on us.
God who changed water into wine at a wedding,
Fill all who thirst with the free gift of the water of life,
God whose light shines like a bright guiding star have mercy on us.

Pause to offer up your own intercessions.

Lord God Almighty, thank you that Jesus' epiphany as Son of God reaches across time and space. As we go into this day may we embrace your call to come and see, come and follow, go and tell others. May we remember that we are bearers of Christ's light sent out to touch others so that they may know him as Son of God and experience the hope his message brings.

Go into the world knowing you are led by the light that is Christ,
May the love of the Creator go before you,
May the life of the Redeemer be within you,
May the joy of the Sustainer shine through you,
This day and evermore,
Amen.

About the Authors

Susan Wade and her husband served as missionaries with Mennonite Mission Network in Taiwan and Hong Kong for 14 years. She currently teaches history at Horizon Christian School in Hood River, OR where she is enjoying the beauty of the Columbia River Gorge, the sense of community to be found in a small town, and a slower pace of life – for now, at least.

Ricci Kilmer lives with her husband and three children in Seattle, Washington. For some time she has been interested in combining faith with the practicality of daily life. In 2010 she integrated her love of food and desire for justice into a resource entitled *Justice at the Table*.

Christine Sine is Executive Director of Mustard Seed Associates. She speaks and writes about how to integrate spiritual rhythms into everyday life as well as on spirituality and gardening. Christine and her husband Tom and their golden retriever Bonnie love practicing hospitality and cooking food from all over the world. They particularly enjoy teaching people how to party the kingdom 24/7. Her most recent book is *To Garden with God*. She blogs at http://godspace.wordpress.com.

Other MSA Resources

E-books and Media

To Garden with God
by Christine Sine

A manual for backyard organic gardening prepared by Chritine Sine for spring workshops. This resource mixes practical advice with spriitual reflections on creation and God's great bounty.

Turbulent Times – Ready or Not!
by Tom Sine

In these changing economic times, how can churches and individuals better respond to the needs of vulnerable neighbors and be good stewards of their resources?

Justice at the Table
by Ricci Kilmer

This resource is a collection of personal reflections and practical ideas to help us redeem "food" in all its dimensions – from its mundane place as an annoying chore to a spiritual practice essential to a life of faith. Take a look and see how you can continue to redeem your relationship with food for the kingdom of God.

A Journey Into Wholeness: Lenten Reflection Guide
by Christine Sine

A five-week study with reflections, litanies, and activities exploring our brokenness and the suffering of Jesus Christ as he jouneyed toward the cross.

A Journey Into God's Resurrection-Created World: An Easter Celebration Guide
by Christine Sine

Advent Reflection Videos
by Christine Sine

Every year, Christine creates another meditation on the coming of Christ. Titles include "The Coming of the Lord Is Near," "Waiting for the Light," and "Awaiting the Christ Child." Available at stores.lulu.com/mail1058

Recordings from Past Events

Did you miss our conferences the past few years? For just a couple of bucks you can hear from Shane Claiborne, Efrem Smith, Lisa Domke, Mark Scandrette, Eliacin Rosario-Cruz, just to name a few. Available at stores.lulu.com/mail1058

Books by MSA Staff
Available at www.msainfo.us

Godspace: Time for Peace in the Rhythms of Life
by Christine Sine (Barclay Books, 2006)

Living on Purpose: Finding God's Best for Your Life
by Christine and Tom Sine (Baker Books, 2002)

Travel Well: Maintaining Physical, Spiritual, and Emotional Health During International Ministry
by Christine Aroney-Sine, M.D. (World Vision, 2005)

Tales of a Seasick Doctor
by Christine Aroney-Sine, M.D. (Zondervan, 1996)

The New Conspirators: Creating the Future One Mustard Seed at a Time
by Tom Sine (InterVarsity Press, 2008)

Mustard Seed vs McWorld: Reinventing Life and Faith for the Future
by Tom Sine (Baker Books, 1999)

Made in the USA
Charleston, SC
09 November 2011